Cynthia Christensen

Restorative Grief A guide to healing the birthmother's heart

Cynthia Christensen

Cynthia Christensen

ISBN-10: 0692453164
ISBN-13: 978-0692453162

ACKNOWLEDGEMENTS

I would like to thank my children, Kasey and Noah, and my husband, Eric for their graciousness and patience while I trudged once again through the grief of my adoption experience to convey the message in this book. I would also like to thank my Grandma, Tippy Arnold, for praying that I would get caught every time I did something wrong. Without you, I may not have written this book!

Cynthia Christensen

CONTENTS

Cynthia Christensen

1 YOU'RE HOME, NOW WHAT?

RIGHT NOW, you are probably feeling like you are dying. Your arms are feeling empty and your heart is feeling shattered. Your mind is racing – intent on finding a solution for the grief, something to make it stop hurting immediately. You have so many different emotions running through your body right now that you don't even know which to focus on. Maybe you don't want to focus on one for too long because of the intense pain it brings with it. One thing I hope will give you comfort is that you are not alone! Hopefully, that statement will become more and more evident to your as you go through this book, even though reading it right now does not bring immediate relief.

Being a birthmother myself, I would venture to guess that you are feeling many, possibly all, of these:

Despair/Desperation	Separation
Loneliness	Fear
Frustration	Emptiness
Numbness	Guilt
Depression	Anger
Jealousy	Disappointment
Helplessness	Brokenness

There may be many things you are feeling that are not on the list above. What I ask of you is to dig deep to find every emotion you are feeling, even though this will hurt. Then write them all down so that you may address every emotion throughout this study. The path to wholeness after adoption will not be easy, but it will be well worth it!

Think back with me to the time before you found out you were pregnant. What did your life look like then? How did you feel about yourself? Were you struggling or were you completely happy with yourself and your life? I would have given anything even to feel like I did before having my dear baby. Choosing adoption and being in the middle of living it out hurt too much. Now that I am on the other side of adoption, I see that I was broken, hurting, and struggling even before I got pregnant. I am post-adoption and more complete than I have *ever* been. That, sweet girl, is the reason I am writing this book.

You can be there, too. You can come out of this adoption more complete than you ever thought possible. That is why God inspired me to write this book: *for you and you alone!* That is the good news I was told to bring you! Although like the actual adoption, with this comes the challenge of letting God work through your pain *with* you – to bring you in to complete wholeness!

There is no detour around the pain in grief. The only way past it is through it. Yes, this probably hurts worse than anything you have experienced, but it is the only way to get *completely* past the grief. If you leave any part of this grief behind and don't deal with it, it will resurface continuously. I'm not saying you will never have grief over adoption ever again, but when the grief comes again, you will be better equipped to handle it and to speak truth into your thoughts. Also, as time passes, the grief will come less and less often if you have an effective way to handle it. Unresolved grief will keep you from your full potential in this life, and will also cause constant little twinges of pain until it is fully dealt with. I don't know about you, but I did not want those constant little painful episodes, so I addressed everything I was feeling no matter how painful. You *will* feel happy again if you do this! It *is* hard work, but you can do this. You are a strong woman and you've proven that by making the most unselfish decision imaginable.

While I hope this book helps with the grieving process, more importantly I hope it helps you to rest in the arms of your Father God while He and He alone nurtures and comforts your broken soul. Isaiah 61 tells us that God sent Jesus to comfort us who mourn and provide for us who grieve, to bestow on us a crown of beauty instead of ashes, oil of gladness instead of mourning, and a garment of praise instead of a spirit of despair. He promises!

The Bible is full of promises like these, but I challenge you to own this one right this second – even if you have a hard time believing it! Take a chance on it and just *choose* to believe that this verse is speaking about you. Because the last part of this verse says, "We (you and I, honey) will be called oaks of righteousness, a planting of the Lord for the display of His splendor." You are the daughter of a King and your King takes pleasure in you and is proud of you!

Something I would really like to encourage you to do is to keep a journal. Use it to write down notes and thoughts from this study, but also as a prayer journal. Then look back on it occasionally and see how God has answered and kept His promises to make you whole again. Another thing I encourage is for you to do one chapter a week, just to let the healing tools of each chapter soak deeply into your soul. Feel free to do whichever chapter you may need any given week.

Let's take a look at the wide range of emotions you may be feeling, including the meanings of some of them. We will address each one of these in more depth in the chapters to follow.

DESPAIR: To despair can be described as a complete and total abandonment of hope that leaves the mind apathetic or numb. I remember feeling this physically. Maybe you know what I am talking about…the pain inside that makes us feel like we are dying. Our bodies actually hurt. Despair is the emotional pain that shows up and actually makes our bodies hurt. *Badly.*

LONELINESS: Loneliness can be described as being sad from a lack of companionship and/or sympathy. In your case, probably both a lack of companionship *and* sympathy. I know that I sure felt lonely, but only lonely for one person – a little bundle of beautiful named Joshua. No one else on the face of this earth could have replaced him, although sometimes I wanted to be close to him so badly that I thought of calling his birthfather and asking him to come over. He was the closest thing I had to my baby boy. I had been in an on-again, off-again relationship with my son's father for many years. He and I had always had a very special connection but he struggled with addictions that would have been detrimental to my child's well-being. That was my main reason for choosing adoption. If you are not together with the birthfather anymore, I encourage you to stand firm and not give in to this temptation. It is very destructive and only complicates and intensifies the pain even more. My challenge to you is to wait until you have finished this study to engage anyone in a relationship. Ideally, it would be best if you did not engage anyone in a relationship until God leads you in that direction. You will be thankful for that decision in the end. Addressing the issue of sympathy, unless you are friends with another birthmother or a woman who has ever lost a child, you are probably feeling like the sympathy you are getting just doesn't match your situation. I remember this making me angry. I felt like no one could even come close to understanding the depth of the pain I had, and wished they wouldn't even try.

EMPTINESS: Emptiness is defined as "being marked by the absence of human life, activity, or comfort" according to *The Merriam-Webster Collegiate Dictionary*[1]. So much is said in that one little sentence. I remember feeling empty even before adoption became a part of my life. After adoption, I felt hollow, minus the heart inside of me. I could feel my heart break with each beat. Keep in mind, however, that just as an empty vase has more room for living, fragrant flowers, the emptiness inside you also has much potential for life changing fragrance; the fragrance of Christ, restoration, and healing.

DEPRESSION: "A…disorder marked especially by sadness, inactivity, difficulty in thinking and concentration, a significant increase or decrease in appetite and time spent sleeping, feelings of dejection and hopelessness, and sometimes suicidal tendencies," as defined also by *The Merriam-Webster Collegiate Dictionary*[2]. Even this may seem an understatement to some. I would describe it as a feeling of drowning in a sea during a hurricane. I don't believe that the depression was of its own. I believe it came as a result of all the other emotions. I also believe that much, if not all, of our depression can be resolved if we deal with our "cracks" instead of super-gluing them quickly to relieve the pain. It does hurt, but it certainly also helps.

DISAPPOINTMENT: Are you feeling disappointed at your life and how it is turning out? Disappointed at the decisions you have made that led up to this point? Maybe disappointed because you feel like you've let others down…including yourself. This is just not how you expected your life to play out, right? That is how I felt too. Like I had let my parents down and the list went on and on. I have always felt a higher standard from my stepfather because he chose to love me and stick with me even though he didn't have to. I still hate to think of letting him down! I believe the devil *loves* this emotion because it is a game board to him. He can burn this emotion into your soul like a tattoo; causing you to constantly describe yourself as a disappointment or a failure. I *caution* you to avoid this mistake because it is not an accurate view. Our mistakes do not equal our worth. God extends His grace to us. If you encounter (and you probably will) people who will not forgive you for this or look down on you for your decision, just know that it is something within them; an unresolved issue or attitude. Something inside them is in bondage. Don't let others decide your worth based on that! Let God! Let God show you how much you are worth, and then choose to believe it! OWN IT!

SEPARATION: In order to separate something, what has to happen? A whole unit has to be divided. When you were pregnant, you and your baby were a whole unit. You functioned together, felt every emotion together, ate and smiled together for nine entire months. At birth, the doctor severed the umbilical cord. This is not physically felt by mother or baby. At a birth where adoption is occurring, however, severing the umbilical cord means so much more. The severing is so symbolic to the damage that is done in the mother's heart. I remember thinking I was so ready to be done being pregnant and ready to meet my new little life but at the same time wishing I could stop time because I knew the true separation was about to occur.

How do you emotionally separate yourself from a life you grew inside you for months on end? Going home, I felt the separation worse because my arms were empty. I couldn't even look into my baby's face for comfort. I found myself wondering constantly what he was doing and how he was. This hurts you, I know. Believe me, if I were there right now, I would hug you like there is no tomorrow!

FEAR Are you afraid of what you are feeling? Afraid of where you go from here? Afraid of your baby being in a home where he isn't loved like you planned for him/her? Fear is an emotion we all have; some of us continually live in it. Fear is also an emotion straight from the pit of hell. The devil loves for us to live in fear, because it holds us back from the mighty potential God gave us. This is contrary to how we are to live, though. God began this process with you whether you were aware of it or not. His hand is always at work in your life and your baby's life. He is here for you through this adoption because you are His child and He loves you! Open the Bible up, sweet girl. It is full of promises from your Father.

Isaiah 41:10 says, "So do not fear, for I am with you; do not be dismayed, for I am your God. I will strengthen you and help you; I will uphold you with my righteous hand."

The Bible is full of *promises* from God to *you!* Own this verse as yours.

NUMBNESS: This is defined in the *Merriam-Webster Collegiate Dictionary* as being "devoid of sensation or emotion."[3] I felt numb to anything happy. Nothing, and I mean *nothing* brought me joy for what felt like an eternity. It was almost as if I didn't feel worthy of having joy. I felt like nothing was joyous without my baby. What I didn't realize at the time was that by having that attitude, I was holding myself back from the victory that God had already given me but I hadn't yet accepted. Satan had a grip on me by telling me that I shouldn't be happy because what I had done was bad and I was bad. By my thinking on those negative thoughts, I was living in bondage to my past. God wants everyone involved in adoption to become whole again *and* experience victory. That includes *feeling* all the happy, joyful emotions life has to offer!

ANGER: I was mad at the world! I was mad at the people who hadn't messed up like I had. I was mad at myself for getting into this mess. I was mad at anyone who tried to be nice to me because I felt like no amount of niceness could make up for how horrible I was feeling! I was mad at the adoptive parents for being happy to take my baby home, I was mad that they brought a gift to the hospital for me, because it could never compare to the gift I gave them! I was one mad girl! In reality, if I truly broke my anger down to the root, I was mad that I had allowed myself to get into that situation. What I later learned is that just like I was overreacting to being angry at all those around me, I had to give myself a break also. I had made a mistake. I had gotten myself into a horrible situation. That did not mean I was a horrible person or that I needed to stay continually angry at myself. It simply meant that I needed to learn from my mistakes and use them to grow into a woman who made better choices. An important aspect in moving forward after adoption is to stop being angry at yourself and putting yourself down. Sometimes our actions are not lovable and they are angering, but we need to learn to separate ourselves from that and grow in the identity that Christ has given us. Then, as we do that, our behaviors will begin to match our new identity.

HELPLESS: You are undoubtedly feeling this as you read these words. You feel helpless to make the pain go away, helpless to go on, helpless to hold your baby. Helpless is defined as the inability to help oneself; dependent. You were there the day you were born! Please know that this emotion has been a constant since your entry into this world. You are just consciously experiencing it right now. We will find ourselves helpless to many situations throughout our lives. The good thing about this emotion is that it isn't as bad as it sounds or feels to you right now. Actually, my hope for you is that by the end of this study, you are at peace because you *know* you are helpless! It sounds crazy but it is *so incredibly* freeing when you finally realize that God is ultimately in control and you learn to just surrender to Him.

DEATH: I remember feeling like I was very close to death as I was leaving the hospital. I remember feeling the despair and surrender one feels when facing the end of their journey. I felt that way because my intense emotional pain seemed to be manifesting itself physically. I could actually feel pain in my body. Everything in me hurt. I hurt worse than I ever had in all my life. Moving hurt, thinking hurt, just existing hurt. This is a normal reaction. Don't worry that you are truly dying. Your body is not going to quit on you. What *is* happening is that you are experiencing a death. This goes back to the severing of the umbilical cord. You are suffering the death of a child. Not that this child is dead to you or is going to die; but when a mother is separated from a child in any way, shape, or form, a kind of death does occur. God gave us mommy hearts and all they want to do is love and nurture our babies. A mommy, is a mommy, is a mommy. We were created for that! Your heart knows that and it grieves like it is experiencing a death. This is a very heartbreaking thing for everyone involved. Just know that out of every death, springs the hope of life – and dare to dream that you will get to a whole new level of life after you have mourned *for a time.* Not for all your life!

Ecclesiastes 3:1, 4 says, "There is a time for everything, and a season for every activity under heaven…a time to weep and a time to laugh, a time to mourn and a time to dance."

FRUSTRATION: If you are anything like I was, you are frustrated at the permanency of this situation, the lack of painless options, or maybe even your lack of discretion in choosing a sex partner. I felt all of those things and more! By being frustrated, we are just keeping ourselves in bondage longer. Even though we feel frustration, it is a useless emotion. It is a springboard to negativity. Usually our frustrations are things we cannot change *or* control so we have to just *choose* to not allow frustration to stay around for long.

GUILT: This is a tool the devil keeps close at hand and he is willing to use it at the drop of a hat. Your job with this emotion is to fight it, resist it! We have all been guilty at some point in our lives of something and we all will be again. We were not created to live in continual guilt. However, Satan loves it when we do. We have to always keep our eyes open for guilt and condemnation. If and when you are guilty of something, the best thing to do is acknowledge it to God, tell Him you are sorry, try your absolute hardest (with prayer and leaning on God) to learn from it and not do it again…and then, be done with it. Nothing is so bad that you won't be forgiven by your Father God. NOTHING. There is no magic number that God waits for you to get to so He can quit forgiving your mess-ups. There is forgiveness every single time you ask.

JEALOUSY: This is another one of those emotions I recall vividly! I was so incredibly jealous of Joshua's adoptive parents. They were going to get to hit all the major milestones with him. That produced pure jealousy inside me. Jealousy is not an emotion from God, but it is a reality. Another that we must face and conquer quickly every time we feel it or it will overtake us with negative garbage. When this emotion creeps in, start meditating on, and even writing down all the blessings in your life…on what you *do* have. Thank God that you aren't where you used to be and/or thank Him for where He is taking you. By developing a thankful heart, even if you have to start out small, you will begin to squelch the all too human emotion that is jealousy.

BROKENNESS: I won't say too much about this because I *know* you are feeling this and it will be something we constantly address in this study. Because the ultimate goal to healing the pain of adoption is healing the brokenness, let's just call this our ultimate goal. What is the opposite of broken? Maybe whole? And what's another word for whole? Complete? Let's go…

2 EMPTY ARMS

BECAUSE OF adoption, I would bet the baby you carried for months was a heavy burden, both physically and emotionally. Now, that's not to say you don't love your child and didn't cherish your pregnancy, but you were faced with the end everyday. The word adoption probably haunted you all of those months. That's a heavy load that you probably would have traded in a heartbeat. I remember how tiring it was thinking of that moment after delivery when I had to hand my baby over to another mother.

When leaving the hospital, physically you weigh less. Emotionally, you carry more weight than you ever have. You are carrying a load that not many could withstand and few ever choose. You *chose* this knowing it would be painful.

Undoubtedly, it was because you have intense love

for your child and you knew that you had the strength deep inside you to conquer your pain. Now, with your arms empty, you must remember and find that strength inside you again. I know you aren't feeling strong right now at all, but God promises in Psalm 29:11, "The Lord gives strength to His people; the Lord blesses His people with peace." Just in case you were wondering, you *are* His! We are all His creation and ultimately, He desires for us all to accept Him as our Lord and Savior and walk in complete fellowship with Him!

Psalm 73:26 says, "My flesh and my heart may fail, but God is the strength of my heart and my portion forever." Our flesh sometimes gets us into situations that may lead us to adoption. That is how it happened for me. I had allowed my flesh to run my life until that point. I felt that God wasn't big enough to help me get control over my desires. Because my flesh was weak, it also weakened my heart. It broke my heart into tiny shards because I had to tell my little boy goodbye in an effort to give him more. At that point, all I could do was look to God. Right then I realized all I could rely on was *His* strength. My arms were empty; my body expected the cries of a baby wanting to nurse…and there was nothing. This feeling caused me to want to run. Not physically run, but get rid of the pain. However, it is especially not going to go away if you run and don't allow yourself to deal with the emotion. So what I encourage you to do is feel it. Feel the pain of not being able to hold your baby, the pain of not being able to look into his or her eyes, hear all of the little noises and cries. Don't ignore or stuff those feelings; address them.

A journal excerpt from my time in this pain says, "I hate everything right now. I feel like I am drowning and even though I don't want to, I don't have the strength to fight it anymore. I am tired. Please carry me, I'm begging you." That was my prayer. It was a desperate one. That prayer gives the visual of a woman on her knees at the end of her rope, a woman at the end of herself, a woman willing to do anything to survive. That's what I saw with my earthly eyes. My Father God saw His daughter in a moment of unbearable pain crying out in agony but with a future of prosperity and healing. I know it is hard for you to imagine a prosperous future for yourself right now, but by taking steps to fully heal and draw close to the Lover of your soul, healing is only a moment away.

Take this time in your life minute by minute if you have to. Take the good with the bad and ask Jesus to reveal Himself and His plan for you. Jeremiah 29:11 says, "For I know the plans I have for you,' declares the Lord, 'plans to prosper you and not to harm you, plans to give you hope and a future." You are not an accident and your future will not come on accident either. Trust in Him.

Have you ever experienced a time when you wished you were a little kid again and could just hop up on your mom's or dad's lap and get some good ol' snuggle time? Just for comfort? Try that this week with your *Heavenly* Father. Instead of focusing on not being able to hold your baby this week, focus on letting your Father hold you and comfort you. As much as you want to comfort your little one, how much more does your Father want to comfort you!

You no doubt need it, but you also deserve it. You can rest assured that God plans to bring you full circle into healing. So my challenge to you right now is to feel the pain, but at the same time, look to God for comfort. Climb up into His lap, curl up, and rest. By that, I mean get into your Bible, pray, and talk to God all day about *every* emotion that you feel. Those restful moments with Him will give you the strength to press on through all the pain. Make time for many restful moments with your Savior. Talk to Him; speak to Him in your purest fashion. Be real with Him. Write out your prayers daily in your journal and watch Him begin answering you.

You can't stop crying? I couldn't either. If you're anything like me, you don't like others seeing you cry. I will go to great lengths to hide my tears from people. Guess what? Jesus doesn't mind if you cry in His presence. Lose it with Him. He feels your pain with you and can comfort you much better than anyone on this earth can. I felt that if I started crying, I just wasn't going to be able to stop. Some experts will tell you that tears cause certain brain chemicals to be released that are pain relievers. Do you think this is by accident? No way! My guess is that the Creator of all things planned it that way! Crying in grief is okay and necessary! Allow yourself to do it; better yet, do it in the arms of your Father God.

I understand that many people will not be able to relate and it may make them slightly uncomfortable to be around you, especially if you are crying. The important thing to remember is that this is *your* healing. This is *your* time and you need to show yourself as much love as you have shown your child.

Reverse the situation for a minute. How would you want your child to treat themselves if he/she were in your shoes? What would you want their opinion of themselves and their future to be? Would you want them to fully heal and emerge a new and beautiful creation in Christ? If so, you should want the same for yourself. God wants the same for you!

Why did you choose adoption even though you knew it would be painful?

____

____

____

____

____

____

____

____

How do you feel about the concept of just allowing yourself to cry? Why?

____

____

____

____

Now let's write out the following verses and truly think about their words.

Psalm 63:8:

____

____

____

____

____

____

____

In this verse, it says that His hand will uphold you. Many here on earth may have failed you in this area. You probably can't think of too many people who have continually lifted you up and not let you down. No human can. God can, though.

Romans 5:3:

____

____

____

____

____

____

____

This verse says that we should rejoice in our sufferings. I don't know about you, but the pain I felt was no cause for rejoicing. You have to *choose* to rejoice. Your mind will catch up later. Think about the rewards of your suffering – perseverance, character, and hope. How does that sound to you?

Psalm 126:5:

___

___

You, girl, will reap with songs of joy!

Isaiah 25:8:

___

___

___

___

___

___

___

He and He alone wants to wipe away the tears from your face.

2 Corinthians 1:3-7:

___

___

___

___

___

____

____

____

____

He is the ultimate Comforter and He teaches us how to comfort others that are in our situations. You are a vessel that God can use! No matter what your past is, He plans on using you by growing you! If that were not the case, I wouldn't have written this book!

Psalm 30:5:

____

____

____

____

____

____

This addresses two issues. Have you ever felt like God can't forgive you for something? Maybe even in this situation? You've got His favor for a lifetime! Your weeping may remain for a night, but rejoicing comes in the morning. Hope is new every day! Every minute! Every second, if need be! He will meet you right where you are.

Isaiah 40:31:

____

____

____

____

____

____

____

He will renew your strength each and every time you need it! So that you will run the race of life and not grow weary; walk and not be faint! Praise God!

Habbakuk 3:19:

____

____

____

____

____

____

____

____

Are you getting it yet? You don't have the strength in yourself to complete the race of healing (and I mean a healthy, full-circle, freeing kind of healing!) from your adoption. God, however, does. He has the strength you need and He offers it freely! Don't get me wrong, people do heal from adoptions even if they don't have God. The question is, do you want to just heal enough to get by, or do you want to heal *and* thrive for the rest of your life? Be the best you can be. Win the race that's been set out for you!

I encourage you to write the previous verses out more often if you need the reassurance and to help you remember them when you aren't feeling so strong. Meditate on them daily to help build up your strength. Talk to God about *everything*, even if you think it is bad and don't want Him to know you are thinking it. That scripture about the truth setting you free is accurate. The best way to rid yourself of bad junk coming in to your mind is to tell God and allow Him to work with it. He is an artist, ready to turn your junk into a beautiful creation!

Let's write out this final verse for the chapter.

Philippians 4:8-9:

____

____

____

____

____

Keep a steadfast heart, my girl, and peace and fellowship with God shall be all yours!

3 WHO IS RAISING MY BABY?

JESUS WAS raised by a mother and father that were not biologically His. They were just vessels God used to bring light into the world. Every child brings light. Every child comes with a purpose. Jesus was not only a blessing to the world but also to first-time parents, Mary and Joseph.

Let's put the focus on them for a minute. Jesus was their first born. They weren't married when they found out they were pregnant (even though they had not sexually conceived Jesus). They were inexperienced parents. Do you think they got parenting Jesus 100 percent right?

I don't think they were perfect parents, but they were the perfect parents for the job. Much pressure is put on adoptive parents to be better than "normal" parents because they have to jump through hoops to prove they can do it. Birthparents don't have to do that. Sometimes birthparents worry about the couple they are choosing. Sometimes birthparents have unrealistic expectations about how perfect their couple is or how perfect they should be.

I am willing to bet that adoptive mother Mary had her fair share of mommy mess-ups! Think about this for a moment: Jesus was twelve years old when they went to Jerusalem for the Feast of the Passover. When the Feast was over, Mary, Joseph, friends and family loaded up and headed home. Still traveling home a day later, they realized Jesus wasn't with them. They had been careless and assumed he was among them. Then when they went back for Him, they didn't find Him for three days. Imagine the panic these two parents felt! Especially having to travel for an entire day just to get to the place they saw Him last. They knew God saw all and they did not know how God was going to react. How humbling! All was well once they found Him, and all along it was God's will, but they had to have been scared of God's reaction to them losing His only Son! The very child He chose them to parent! He knew; even before choosing them to be Jesus' parents.

Would you as a birthmother choose someone you knew would lose your child for a few days? *All* parents mess up sometimes. We have to learn to be compassionate and understanding when we choose our baby's parents, even as we watch them mess up sometimes. Mary's house probably wasn't even kid-proofed! Surely, Jesus drank the donkey shampoo at least once! But guess what? God still said, "Mary, you are chosen, You will be Jesus' earthly mother." He saw her every move, every thought, every fault, and still He chose her!

My hope is that you chose your adoptive parents very carefully and prayerfully. Adoption is a beast to navigate in and of itself and relationships can get complicated if there is any deceitfulness or secrecy as its foundation. Proverbs 19:21 says, "Many are the plans in a man's heart, but it is the Lord's purpose that prevails." There could come a time in the future where you look back and aren't so confident of your choice. If that should happen, meditate on the above scripture and trust that the Lord is working it all out.

Even if you know they are the right ones, you may see a glimpse of their inadequacies at times. I can tell you that after giving birth, when the adoptive parents I chose came to the hospital, I was worried out of my mind! They were so nervous that they couldn't change Joshua's diaper; they had not the slightest clue on how to take care of a newborn child! Now, I knew my baby would be watched over by God, but man, was I concerned! I said lots of prayers and hoped that they would relax and not be so on edge. I came from a family that had babies around all the time so parenting came very naturally for me. It was hard to understand these parents!

Adoptive parents have to go through the wringer to even be considered for a baby. Please understand that if they seem to be trying too hard, it's because they are. They are working tirelessly for their hearts' desire. They want you to like them and they are afraid for you to see anything less than perfection because if you do, you might not choose them. This is where God works. This is where God asks you to take a step back and accept exactly what you see in front of you, faults and insecurities and all. That's what He does with us! So who are we to judge more critically than our own Father God? This is just true with everyone we encounter in life, not just adoptive parents.

Sometimes we get caught up in righteousness, though, and begin to think, "I wouldn't do that, I would do it differently, I would do it better." When we start thinking that way, it's time to pray and ask for forgiveness. What's going on with baby and adoptive parents is between them and God once we have relinquished our rights. The very definition of "relinquishing rights" confirms the reality. We as birthparents have no more rights. That is why it is *imperative* that you have thought this entire thing out completely before actually choosing adoption. It isn't going to be picture perfect and it really isn't a better option it's just a different option.

Psalm 71:5-6 says, "For you have been my hope, O sovereign Lord, my confidence since my youth. From birth I have relied on you; you brought me forth from my mother's womb. I will ever praise you." Just because it isn't our way doesn't mean it's not *a* right way. Don't forget, however, that this is also the time He asks the adoptive parents to trust Him and let their inadequacies be seen. In a sense, He asks everyone on both sides of the equation to be transparent. Let's look at a few verses from the Bible.

Isaiah 26:4 says, "Trust in the Lord forever, for the Lord, the Lord, is the Rock eternal."

John 14:1 says, "Do not let your hearts be troubled, Trust in God; trust also in Me (Jesus)."

Psalm 28:7 states, "The Lord is my strength and my shield; my heart trusts in Him, and I am helped. My heart leaps for joy and I will give thanks to Him in song."

Do you see the word that appears in all these verses? *Trust.* Trust is hard for many of us, especially those of us who are broken. However, it is essential for making your relationship with your baby and his/her adoptive parents work. Consider this for a moment: the whole relationship between you, your baby, and the adoptive parents is a circle. In the middle of that circle is God. The whole deal requires God at the center, to be the core around which all else is built.

The baby relied on you while you were pregnant for its well-being. Now you must rely on Jesus for your own well-being. You have to trust that your baby *is* a blessing, no matter what your circumstances were in getting pregnant. You had to have recognized that by the fact that you did not make the choice for abortion. Now you need to realize that you are a blessing to God. You are His child. Your child is His child. Even when you are not present, He is still watching over your child. You are both His. Trust that though the adoptive parents are only human and not super-parents, they will do, because it isn't about them. It's about your child. It's between your child and God and the plan for your child's life was set in place long before you even knew you were pregnant.

Isaiah 48:17 says, "…I am the Lord your God, who teaches you what is best for you, who directs you in the way you should go."

God believed in Mary and Joseph. They weren't millionaires. They couldn't take Jesus to do and see all the coolest things of the times. They couldn't dress him in designer smocks and sandals. They couldn't guarantee anything, except that they would be faithful and loving all of His days on earth. There were days they were upset with Him, there were days He was just a typical child doing typical child things. As His parents, however, they loved Him everyday. Period.

That is what I tell my children all the time. I love you period. Even when you seem unlovable, I still love you, and so does Jesus. Mary and Joseph were simply vessels trying to do their best as His parents. It is my assumption that all adoptive parents are going to try their best to be good parents or they would not have applied for adoption in the first place. God equips the called, not the other way around. So, assuming God's hand is in your adoption, He will protect your child. He equipped Mary and Joseph. He handed His only Son over to imperfect people to raise. He was *perfect*, and still He chose imperfection.

Moses was born into dire circumstances. His mother loved him dearly but knew that if he was discovered he would be killed in an effort to control the Israelite population. She hid him away for three months, until she could no longer conceal him, and then she put him in a papyrus basket and sent him down the river. She did not know if this fate would be any better or worse than his fate if she kept him. Her faith and love carried her. Pharaoh's daughter found baby Moses and felt sorry for him. She, however, could not feed him, so she sent for a Hebrew woman to nurse the baby. That Hebrew woman was Moses' mother. She returned Moses when he was older and he was raised by Pharaoh's daughter. She watched her Hebrew son be raised in a powerful family and go on to do mighty things for the Lord. I can actually *feel* this mother's heartache as she watches her beloved son grow. I picture her peeking over a fence, looking into her child's life, aching to be reunited with him, but also doting over the man he was becoming because of the choice she had made. I also imagine her praying daily to be reunited with Moses, if not in this life then in the life to come.

That is my prayer. Eternity with my baby…Dare to dream big for your baby. Dare to dream of your child's soul being soaked in the grace and love of God until he or she makes it to the place of eternity. There, in that place, there are no more goodbyes.

After relinquishment, we can and still should pray for our babies every day. We should not only pray for their physical safety here on this earth, but for their souls to crave and race toward God for the finish line of Eternity. If they make it and so do we, we will get to look into our children's eyes everyday forever. That makes this little jaunt here on earth seem like nothing. That reduces your decision to relinquish to just a season, not forever.

Rest in the Lord your God. Know that His plan is perfect. He wants the best for everyone involved, because everyone involved is a child of His! Don't be afraid. There is pain in embracing the adoptive family as extended family but there is more pain in not doing that. Let God lead you as to how open your adoption is, but no matter what, the more solid you can make this relationship, the more trust you put in it, the better off your baby will be. Abundant blessings will come from allowing kindness and compassion to infiltrate your interactions with the adoptive parents. Trust, trust, trust.

4 GOD IS AN ADOPTIVE PARENT? REALLY?

READ EPHESIANS 1:3-14. Write out what it means to you:

We have the opportunity to be God's adopted children! Isn't this just a gem of scripture? If hugs (the great big, squeezy kind) were manifested in words, these would be the ones! This is God putting His seal (Holy Spirit) in each and every one of us! He wants us to ask Him into our hearts, confess our sins to Him, and turn from our negative behaviors. (At the end of this book, there is a prayer for you to pray to ask Jesus into your heart.) The best part of it is that we can *all* get the seal, in spite of the messes of our lives!

When we ask Jesus into our hearts, our lives don't magically transform into perfect little existences, right? We have to continue striving toward the goal of transformation in God. It's not a big, giant leap; it's just little steps forward every day.

I encourage you to write the above scriptures out on paper. Have some fun with it. Color it, put artwork with it, do whatever to it. Just write it out and put it in a place where you can read it daily. Soak it up, memorize it, and call upon its words when you are feeling discouraged. Not only does this scripture apply to you but it also applies to your dear baby. God has a plan for everyone and that plan is for us to prosper!

These scriptures tell us that we can be blessed in heavenly realms with every spiritual blessing in Christ, and that He *chose* us in Him to be holy and blameless in His sight. He predestined us to be adopted into His family through the death of Jesus. They also tell us that He works everything out in conformity with the purpose of His will. Adoptive parents appreciate the fact that they had nothing to do with "bearing" a child. Have you ever noticed that when babies are placed with their adoptive parents, they immediately provide for all the child's needs, they are 100 percent attentive, they just jump in with both feet and seem almost overly eager? You can tell they are just so grateful for each passing moment with their new baby. We childbearing people tend to take those moments for granted more because we don't have to go through the uncertainty like adoptive parents. Guess what? God is that overly eager parent, waiting to jump into our lives with both feet. We must first give Him permission to do so.

Could you see the eagerness, the excitement, and the desire in the parents you chose for your baby? Did you also witness the moment of pain on their faces…that moment when you see their excitement come full circle as they are looking at you and they begin to realize that they would do *anything* to have a child to call their own, and yet you are choosing adoption for your child? You are voluntarily giving for no other reason than love and love alone. Is it painful? Of course, but love does conquer all. Love always trumps pain. We can never stop pain from being in our lives, but we can always choose love as our pain control.

There is a type of love called Agape love. Maybe you have heard of it before. Agape love is defined as an unconditional, godly kind of love. Some argue that agape love is not possible in earthly beings because we are not perfect and therefore are unable to give perfect love. Most women who have held their own child, fresh from the womb and forever tied to their soul, know a love *very* similar to agape love. How much more does the woman who chooses adoption? As she holds her dear, precious baby for the first and last time all at once, she not only understands agape love, she is living it out.

As a prospective adoptive parent, God also had to deal with a little uncertainty as to whether or not mankind could be adopted as His own. Sounds weird, doesn't it? Yet, it is true. He sent Jesus to redeem mankind, to die on the cross for us so that we could be adopted into God's family. In a way, Jesus was the first birthparent. See, without Jesus' cooperation, not one of us could be adopted into His family and inherit eternity in Heaven. The Bible tells us He did have a choice. Read Luke 4:1-13. This chapter talks about the temptation of Jesus before He came to die on the cross. It says that for forty days, Jesus was tempted by Satan to just accept this earth as His own and forfeit the original plan of dying on the cross. He had a choice! He didn't want to endure the cross! He didn't deserve it! Yet, He knew that if He didn't endure the cross, you would not have the future and hope that His perfect agape love wanted you to have. Isn't that the resounding truth for every birthparent? That is the driving force in most adoptions; agape love for a hope and a future.

God won; He became our adoptive Father. Jesus won; His death saved us. And we won, because we now have a future and a hope. All because God cared and would do anything to save us. Isn't that just like a parent? Our adoption into His family is a one-time event. Being His child is an eternity deal. Let's use this perfect example of adoption to help us run and endure our race.

The price of adoption has decreased considerably since this "first" adoption. Even though adoptive parents nowadays pay upwards of $20,000.00 for just one child, it pales in comparison to the price paid by Jesus. The clincher is that He still would have died on the cross even if it were only for you and no one else. That's how much He loves each and every one of us!

Sometimes we feel like God won't understand something we are going through or that He just couldn't possibly understand how we are feeling, or the depth of those feelings. I know I've felt this way sometimes but, in the end, I always realize that He *does* get it, and that He is right there in the trenches with us during our pain. If you've felt this way toward God about your adoption, I hope this chapter has helped you to realize that He does get it. As Jesus' Father, He watched His only son be literally tortured and put to death. He knew all along that Jesus had the choice of backing out of the deal. As birthmothers, we also had the choice of backing out, and, as we handed our babies over to another family to raise, it felt like the death of a child. What one of us didn't want to back out? Of course we did, but we hoped it was a better plan! As our adoptive Father, God has watched us control our own lives, make our mistakes, and all the while waited for us to return to Him. Will you return to Him now? Will you love your Father with all that is in you? In Him, our stories have hope. Our stories have a future. Our pain will not have been *useless*, but will be *used!* We will not be *used up* but instead we will be *useful*!

Take some time now to pray to your Father God, rest in Him and all that He is. Soak up His goodness and begin to proclaim the victories you have in Him, because our work has only begun. You are loved, baby girl, and He is very proud of you. Your hard work and diligence will be rewarded over and over again. When you feel your strength beginning to waver, lean on Him.

As you were picking the perfect parents for your child, could you see the love and care exuding from each couple? What did that look like?

____

____

____

____

____

____

____

Could you see the eagerness, the excitement, and the desire in them? How did they portray that?

____

____

____

____

____

Did you ever see that eagerness turn to awe when they realized the magnitude of what you were doing?

____

____

____

What is love? Better yet, Who is love?

The Bible tells us that God is Love in 1 John 4:16. That chapter also goes on to tell us that there is no fear in love and that perfect love drives out fear…Let's write those verses out.

1 John 4:16-19:

____

____

____

____

____

____

____

Those verses talk about perfect love. What do you think perfect love is?

____

____

____

5 DESPAIR

DESPAIR IS defined as the utter abandonment of hope that leaves the mind apathetic or numb, a.k.a. emotional pain that makes our bodies actually hurt. Second Corinthians 4:16-18 says, "Therefore, we do not lose heart. Though outwardly we are wasting away, yet inwardly we are being renewed day by day. For our light and momentary troubles are achieving for us an eternal glory that far outweighs them all. So we fix our eyes not on what is seen, but on what is unseen. For what is seen is temporary, but what is unseen is eternal." This should truly be one of the biggest focal points of our lives, in all reality. Focus on what is to come, what is unseen, not what is going on right now. The one thing certain about life is that each and every one of us will experience death. This life is just preparation for that day; the day we look our Heavenly Father in the eyes and give the account of our lives.

Outwardly, even when things are at their best, we

are still wasting away and one day closer to death. Yet inwardly, with Jesus, there is nothing better! He renews our minds daily; I cannot even express how wonderful it has been to have Jesus in my life! If you stick with Jesus, even in the toughest and darkest of days, He will bring you hope and peace, all along the path of life. Having Jesus in your life doesn't give you immunity from problems and distress, but it does help you get through it gracefully and successfully. The best thing about it is that it comes with a 100 percent satisfaction guarantee! I like to think of it as sort of like an exercise video; if you hold up your end of the deal and actually *do* it (which isn't always the most fun), you will see great results. In the end, it's so worth it!

So, let's look up the opposite of *despair*. The word I am looking for is *hope,* and the meaning of *hope* is to cherish a desire with anticipation.[4] Think for a moment about your feelings of despair. Is that what your despair is? Having no desire and no anticipation?

Do you want to find hope again? Do you want to find healing in a whole new way? Seek Him with all you have, with every inch of your being. Undoubtedly, you know the kind of seeking I am talking about because we all, in our need for acceptance and/or love, have sought someone in a sold-out way at some point. Sell out for your Father this time!

At first, seeking Him may feel awkward, daunting, even a bit confusing; but in pouring yourself into this task, your hope will begin to reappear and despair will begin to die off. Despair is like a deep fog looming about, so when it begins to fade away, you will start to see things clearly. Things become more than what you see on the surface, and you see beyond the "right-here-right-now," and into the future. The pain of your despair will gradually become less and less as hope makes its way back in. There will still be times of grief when despair comes knocking but if you keep yourself and your heart guarded, you will recognize the knock and you can turn it away by recalling verses of hope, thoughts about your future, and the identity that your Father God has given you. Another very important key to your recovery is to be gentle on yourself. If you fall, just get back up and try harder the next time. When you fall again, get back up. God will never stop forgiving or loving you. He will *never* turn you away.

Many times in society, hope is circumstantial. We have hope because everything in life is going pretty well for us. It's easy to have hope then, isn't it? The challenge comes during difficult times. In circumstantial hope, often there's an object for our hope. Even more often, especially in broken people, our hope is in the form of the opposite sex. When our hope depends on circumstances, it begins with "if". Our hopes, balanced on factors out of our control, can quickly be dashed.

If you will take the time to build hope in God, it will live deeply and richly in the soils of your soul. It is like fertile ground, producing beautiful fruit both inside you and outside of you. Believe me, people will begin to take notice! God's kind of hope is like a savings account that pays interest. Every time you make a deposit (in the form of growing more in God), the more hope He puts in for when you need it most. The more hope you get from God, the stronger you'll become and the less you'll need to draw on temporary, circumstantial, fleeting hope.

Think about your hope in the past. Where did it come from? Was it fleeting? Was it circumstantial? Did it ever come from a man? Are you ready for hope to be restored that no one can take from you? God wants to take your despair and replace it with unmatched, unparalleled hope; hope so deeply seeded in your soul that no person could ever steal it from you.

I remember not wanting to get out of bed…ever. My despair was so great. My love for my children is so great and yet, after my adoption, I was so enveloped with despair that I struggled to take care of the two children I already had at home. When I did get out of bed, I felt like a living, breathing dead girl. I felt empty and had nothing to offer anyone. All I could think about was my baby boy, what he was doing, if he was alright. At one point, I even remember my mom telling me that if I was going to be so sad that I couldn't take care of my other two kids, I should go get Joshua back. Don't think for a second that I didn't entertain that thought.

What I figured out was that while God would not directly be answering my questions about my son, the only way to true peace and hope was to draw close to Him. By doing that, He gave me peace about each question I had, peace that caused the specifics about my questions to disappear every time I would hear my Father say, "I've got this under control, don't worry," That's what He wants you to do also.

The important thing is that, with each thought that causes you to start "What-iffing," you turn that thought into a positive thought instead. Write your negative thoughts down, and then write down a positive and *believable* statement to replace it. Then, if you keep doing that, you will begin to see how negative thinking alone affects your mood and your everyday life. An accumulation of our bad habits, including thinking patterns, has brought us to this point today. You need to start being aware of what you have to be thankful for, even if it doesn't seem like there's much. Once you become aware of it, you will realize there *is* much in your life to be thankful for.

You hear about people all over the world getting second chances at life after health issues like cancer or heart attacks or other close calls. There are all kinds of stories of near-death experiences and how some come out of these circumstances going, "Thank you God! This is my second chance at life!" Typically, these people have a greater respect for life and living after suffering what they did. Well, this is your second chance at life! You have lost much in your suffering, but you can gain much also. That may be hard to see right now, but take it from me, you will realize this in time. Because you chose adoption, that tells me that you perceived your circumstances to be less than optimal.

Now you have an opportunity to take advantage of your new circumstances. With God's guidance, you can set a new goal and work toward that it. The key is to remember that you *deserve* happiness again, and God desires it for you! However, that may mean choosing happiness in spite of your circumstances. You must rise up off the floor and begin standing tall. God desires you to step out of the mire and into His grace and redemption. You made a heart-wrenching decision that many people wouldn't have the strength to do. To quote Tim Storey, "Let your test become your testimony, and let your mess become your message."[5] Many people will try to hold you back from accomplishing this, but you can do it. Seek God for your identity. Don't be defined by one circumstance in your life. Live on, Baby. If He can make penicillin out of moldy bread, don't you think He can certainly make something out of you?

Imagine for a minute a prostitute out walking the streets. She walks all over the place all the time and sees many things. One night as she's walking along, she sees a poor, old man stumble and fall in the middle of the street. He's obviously hurt, unable to move, and traffic is nearing. Does she decide to help the man or does she immediately think, "I can't help him, I'm a prostitute, I'm too ashamed." She is going to instinctively help the man even though once she gets him to safety he could completely reject her. So when the man looks into the face of the woman that saved his life, will he see a prostitute or an angel? He's going to see past the woman's circumstance to see that she does have a soul and it is more than people see on the outside.

This correlates to the first scripture I gave you in this chapter (2 Corinthians 4:16-18). Look back at it. It says, "…So we fix our eyes not on what is seen, but on what is unseen. For what is seen is temporary, but what is unseen is eternal." Think about it. We can't see each other's souls, so sometimes it is easier for us to judge based on outward appearance and attitude. Try to see others as God sees them. I shake my head as I write that sentence because sometimes it is *so* hard! Nonetheless, it is so completely necessary.

In one way, I hope your adoption experience will give you more compassion for everyone you encounter because we are all fighting some sort of battle every day. Every person on earth has something inside them that is broken, so handle them with care. In another way, please understand that some others don't look at life from this perspective. They also have broken places, and though they may only want to see you for the choices you've made, rise above their opinions. Leave their heads spinning when they realize you are bigger than your choices.

Just as the prostitute in the story needs to believe she is more than just her circumstances, so do you. Also, just for the record, that was just a story; in no way am I calling you a prostitute. I am challenging you to believe that you are not locked in to your circumstances. In a second, you can change the direction your life is taking by making just one initial good decision. Now, obviously, it takes constant dedication to that decision, but it is one initial decision. In the movie, *A Knights Tale*, the lead character William is set on changing his stars (destiny). He is born a peasant but wants to be a knight. Of course, to be a knight one had to be of noble blood. At one point he says, "How did the nobles become noble in the first place? They took it!" This is what God wants you to do. The only difference is that God gives you a new identity freely. Become who God wants you to become, do it with integrity, and don't let anyone stop you or say differently!

Part of your despair is caused by your perception of failure. Do you feel like you've failed?

____

____

____

In what way(s)?

____

____

____

____

____

____

____

Do you feel like you've failed others besides yourself and if so, who?

____

____

____

____

Describe failure in your own words:

____

____

____

____

____

Many times, we see failure as an end. Even more often, we take that ending failure on as our own identity. We describe ourselves based on how we've failed. As I am writing this, let me note that I struggle with this sometimes still. It's a tough one. The timelines of our lives could look just peachy minus a couple of failures, and yet these failures are what we take on. In my opinion, failure doesn't seem to be the period at the end of the sentence, but instead just a comma. A little pause in the story. That is exactly how we *should* view our falls in life. If failure isn't the period at the end of the sentence, it leaves room for…you guessed it: hope! What do you want to come after this comma in your life? You hold the pencil…finish strong. There is, however, someone who wants to be the punctuation at the end of your life's sentence. It's Jesus. Only He doesn't want to be a period; He deserves an exclamation point!

Write out Psalm 62:5:

____

____

____

____

____

____

____

This is the secret: the truest, most genuine, and purest hope will *only* come from our Father God.

Now let's write out Jeremiah 29:11-13:

____

____

____

____

____

____

____

Where is your heart right now concerning despair?

____

____

____

On a level of 1-10, where is your despair? (10 being the most intense) ________________________

Before adoption, what did you see for your future? (Be specific)

Post-adoption, has that future taken on a different look? Why and how?

____

____

____

____

____

____

____

Now, is it necessary that your future look different? Why or why not?

____

____

____

____

____

____

____

____

____

____

____

When giving your reasons in the above question, are any of them reasons that put you down or speak negatively about you? If so, throw those out and answer the question again, kindly. If you stop hating on yourself, is it possible to continue with your future goals? I understand that you will have come out of adoption with a whole new outlook on some things and that may be the reason for changing what your future looks like. However, if your future looks different because of your self-worth, you need to adjust accordingly…giving yourself lots more credit.

I want to help you get the creative juices flowing regarding your future. What I am going to ask of you is to dream big. Dream big because…you deserve it!

My Dreams

What kinds of things do you enjoy doing?

____

____

____

____

____

____

____

If you have a job right now, what is it and do you like it?

____

____

When you allow yourself to dream, where do you see yourself in two years? In five? In ten?

____

____

____

____

____

____

____

____

____

____

____

____

If you were helping someone in the same situation as you, what would you tell them about their future? Would you advise them to stand tall and walk on or stay in the pit because of their mistakes?

____

____

____

____

____

____

Would you want them to be kind to themselves and dream big dreams? ______________________________

Shouldn't you want the same for yourself?__________

Where would your baby want you to be in two years? In five? In ten?

____

____

____

____

____

Would he/she want you to stand tall and walk on or stay in the pit?

____

____

What are some of your talents and skills? Could they be put to use in a career?

____

____

____

____

6 LONELINESS/EMPTINESS

LOOK AT Psalm 25:16 ESV: "Turn to me and be gracious to me, for I am lonely and afflicted." Are you or have you ever felt like this? Many times women choosing adoption are doing so partly because of a failed or failing relationship. Also, many times those same women have felt lonely most of their lives. Even more often, those women felt lonely even while in a relationship with a male. So, to begin this chapter let me tell you that I understand you may be feeling lonely on many levels. I have been there. We tend to notice our loneliness more when we're in pain or bad times.

Psalm 102:7 ESV says, "I lie awake; I am like a lonely sparrow on the housetop." Ever felt like that? I certainly know I have. In the past, did you search out companionship due to loneliness? I did. Now I realize that when I did find a fix (a.k.a. a man) it merely masked my loneliness. I still always felt lonely, whether with someone, in a crowd, or surrounded by friends. I ask you to take your loneliness to God and ask Him to help you find a true and lasting solution for your loneliness. I can tell you that once you find it, loneliness will very quickly lose its grip on you. Think of it as an infection: left untreated it will go on and cause damage, maybe even death. If treated, it's very manageable and completely curable.

Should we rely on others to fix our loneliness? It may seem like the cure is to surround ourselves with people and relationships, but often we find the cure within. It comes in the form of showing love and kindness to ourselves, learning to like who you are and who God created you to be, and fellowshipping with God – quiet time with Him daily. When He keeps you company, even for just fifteen minutes a day, you feel refreshed, and your loneliness turns to the richness of companionship.

Psalm 68:6 ESV tells us that "God settles the solitary in a home; he leads out the prisoners to prosperity, but the rebellious dwell in a parched land." The word *solitary* means being, living, or going alone or without companions.[6] That word is depressing.

Family is not just those we are related to by blood, but also those who we choose to be in a relationship with. This verse is telling us that, though we may feel alone, God intends to bless us with deep and rich relationships, if we allow Him. He has absolutely no desire for you to feel isolated in this life. It is up to us to pray without ceasing and be diligent in whom we allow our fellowship to be with. If we are careless about choosing our "family," we will continue to be lonely. This is quality versus quantity.

While quantity seems like a logical solution to loneliness, quality is the eternal solution.

Part of getting through loneliness is figuring out why you are having this emotion. Much of it for you right now is that your arms are empty and you desire to hold your child close. Can that be remedied by another person? Let's take a look beyond the baby for a minute, because I would be willing to bet this isn't the first time you have experienced loneliness. Generally, the solutions to loneliness are always the same no matter what the cause. Are you lonely because you aren't an outgoing, well-versed conversationalist? Let me tell you, with much embarrassment, this is me. I am that person that would love to relate to you, talk with you, get to know you, but I won't ask too many questions because I assume most peoples' lives are not my business.

Strangely enough God has called me to counsel people, to ask tough questions. Doesn't make sense does it? I'm naturally shy…and He has called me to public speaking. Also, I assume that my business is not anyone else's business, and He's called me to share my story. My other problem is that because I get nervous when conversing, I almost *always* say something stupid. After it's all said and done, all I can do is laugh at the things I've said. I know people walk away from me thinking, "What is wrong with her?" The good news is that there are books out there on getting over this obstacle. I hope one day to read at least one. If you struggle with this, maybe you could also try a book. No matter what though, remember: practice makes perfect.

Maybe you are lonely because you're afraid of rejection? Rejection is tough. It hurts. Many times, it stems from yet another pain from our pasts that caused us to lose our self-confidence and assurance. Our personalities, habits, happiness, contentment, and many other things in life are all shaped by our pasts and whether or not we have dealt with our baggage in a healthy or negative way. That's why it is so important to deal with everything that comes up in our lives.

Life is hard. It takes much passion and consistency to maintain at a happy level, but it is so worth it. Many times we are afraid of rejection because we experienced it in our younger years by those God assigned to stand behind us at all costs. This is sad, but so common. That's why God is the ultimate parent. He is the only one in our lives that will *never* let us down. If you struggle with rejection, please remember that you were purposefully created to be just the way you are. When someone rejects you, take it to the altar of God and leave it for Him. He will help you get through it.

When we are rejected, we tend to internalize it. We assume that the fault is entirely ours, something is severely wrong with us, and we begin to comb through our baggage to fix the problem. However, that is not always necessary. Oftentimes, rejection occurs because of the issues of the other person(s) involved. In cases of rejection, take it to God, and ask Him to show you if something inside you truly does need some modifying.

Maybe you are feeling lonely because you don't know anyone who has chosen adoption, you feel like you are the only one and your family is of no help because they don't seem to get it. I remember this. Look around for support groups. Call the adoption agency you used and ask them for resources for this. They may be able to get you connected to at least one other birthmother to grieve with. It is extremely important to remain committed to healing from this grief, and sharing it even with just one person who has gone through it can help immensely. If the adoption agency has counseling available, use it.

In most families, adoptions are like the elephant in the room. Everyone knows it occurred, but doesn't want to talk about it or doesn't know how to. It is mostly like that in my family, although, with me being so public about mine, I don't expect it to remain that way forever. You should know, though, that many times it is not brought up because others in your family are grieving also. This occurs especially with grandparents. They must process the grief of not having their grandchild just the same as you must process your grief. So do cut them some slack.

After my adoption, I learned that the grief to the grandparents and great-grandparents was very significant. When I was pregnant, I thought my decision only affected me and my children. That is not the case at all. Further down the road, I figured out it had bothered the birthfather, grandparents, and great-grandparents tremendously. Yes, I had completely written birthfather grief off. I figured it didn't bother him at all. I was wrong.

My crisis pregnancy had affected many other lives. My own personal healing was the best-case scenario. At the current time, I can say that there are some who have not processed the adoption grief in a healthy manner, with one indirectly ending up the worst-case scenario. Don't let this happen to you or your family members. I was selfish in thinking that my adoption only affected my children and me. I was so wrapped up in my own grief that I couldn't see that others were grieving also. Open the doors to communication so that any and all that are grieving can heal.

Unfortunately, there is no quick fix. Have you ever said to yourself, "If I could just have ________, I would feel better"? Then you go get whatever "fix" it is and shortly after you realize it wasn't what you needed and it didn't work? Typically, quick fixes end up costing more, whether emotionally, physically, or any combination of the three. Eternal fixes are hard work and require diligence on our part. Sometimes it is tempting just to take the "easy" road. Trust me, when I say "easy," I mean easy for the moment, hard for the long run. Patience and the ability to focus enough to come up with a healthy, lasting solution to our problems will increase our overall sense of happiness with our lives. The payoff on taking the other road, the "hard" road, is lasting. It's genuine. It sticks with us.

I remember an emptiness inside of me that seemed far too big for God. I actually told Him, "I know you are *all* I should need, but you can't fill this.

I need something more than you, something tangible, something here on earth." Yes, that statement is as ugly as it is honest. I thank God that He allows us to be so upfront and honest with Him. His response to me came years later.

In chapter one, I defined emptiness as "being marked by the absence of human life, activity, or comfort," Leaving the hospital the day of my discharge, all of my worth and value were gone. I could not find a trace of them. The spunk I've always had and the tendency for crazy, lighthearted life…gone. Nothing. I could not even try to feel any of those things; I didn't have it in me. The last piece of me was crumbling to ashes as I walked out of the hospital. I saw it and I just knew it would be the end of me.

Now as I look back, I see that it was a blessing to have that last piece turn to ashes. Before, when a piece of me would break, I would try to superglue it back before anyone noticed. What happens when you superglue something? It may be a quick fix but it still leaves evidence of breakage with a crack or chip. As an example, let's say you have a vase that is cracked. Is it useful to hold things? Not really. But let's say you put the most beautiful bouquet of flowers in it. When you picture that, is the crack a distraction from the beauty that is contained within the vase? That is the case with us. I was down to nothing right after my adoption, I thought. Do you know what Jesus said to that? "You may be nothing to the world, but you are everything to me." I was now a blank canvas for Him He can just make us new and glorious, crack-free.

When God begins rebuilding us, crack-free, He also begins putting more of Himself and His beauty (a.k.a. Holy Spirit) in us. And it shows through! That's where you are headed.

Have you ever tried pouring liquid into a cracked container? We all know what happens, right? It seeps out. A container, by nature, is created to hold things. It cannot fulfill its complete purpose if it has even the slightest crack in it. It doesn't matter if it's a small crack or a large one; eventually, the liquid will completely be lost.

Isn't that how we are? We have a hard time maintaining healthy relationships if we are broken. We can't have a whole relationship until we ourselves are whole. We live in a fast, gimme, gimme, gimme kind of world and when we want something, we want it now. We don't like to wait. Most of the time, when we are forced to wait we think we are the only ones having to do it. We get anxious waiting around for the piece of the puzzle that is equal to not being lonely or empty anymore. When the piece doesn't come when we think it should, we take action to find a similarly shaped piece that will do for now.

It's just what we do. When our stomachs are empty, we eat. When our pantries are empty, we buy groceries. It's jut natural to want to solve our own problems. In many ways, this is a very good quality. When our hearts and souls feel empty, however, we can't solve that problem on our own. The missing piece is Christ. We need His help and we need His strength to stay put until we are whole and don't feel lonely or empty anymore.

There's a saying out there that, "we can't fully love one another until we love ourselves." This is true with loneliness also. We cannot be without loneliness until we find the answer to it within ourselves with God's help. When a new relationship only adds to our lives but isn't a requirement, then we are making some progress.

Sometimes changes may require leaving a loved one behind because they aren't going in the direction you desire your life to go. I did this with my son Joshua's birthfather. He and I had been together off and on for many years. I loved him intensely to the very depth of my soul no matter what he did or how he treated me. I prayed constantly for God to change him so that I could stay with him for the rest of my life because I knew without intervention, he would be detrimental to my kids and I.

I knew in my heart that I couldn't stay without drastic changes. I also knew if I could get those changes, I would stay forever. I ended up having to leave. In the depths of my soul, I didn't want to. It broke my heart to the core, and when I think back, the mental picture I have is one similar to the picture of the "Footprints" poem. Only mine is my heels dug into the dirt, leaning back into the palms of Jesus with Him pushing me to my new destination. I was not exactly totally compliant.

Sometimes, change is painful. I understand. I didn't want to leave him, but I wanted God's best for my children. Guess what? I got not only God's best for my children, I got God's best for myself, as well. I got what God knew I needed. The difference was life and death in every sense. It is worth the pain and it ends up being a blessing. Let God bless you. You believed in what was best for your child, now believe in what's best for you.

"My Father, if it is possible, may this cup be taken from me. Yet not as I will, but as you will."

MATTHEW 26:39

Let's go to the past and check our emotions. Think back to times of loneliness…

When?

____

____

____

____

____

____

Why?

____

____

____

____

____

____

____

How did you fix it?

____

____

____

____

____

____

____

Was it a healthy fix or just a band aid?

____

____

____

____

Did you have companionship at the time or not?

____

____

Think about the lonely feelings you may be having right now.

Who or what are you lonely for?

____

____

____

____

____

____

____

Why?

____

____

____

____

____

____

____

What solution do you have for getting through the loneliness?

____

____

____

____

____

____

____

Is your solution a healthy one? Why or why not?

____

____

____

____

____

____

Will it move you closer to healing, postpone it, or completely set it back? Why?

____

____

____

____

____

____

Let's evaluate the relationships in our lives right now. Explain what you like and dislike about each type and then make a course of action (if needed) for getting these relationships up to the level you would like them to be. Only write down the things *you* personally can do to help improve these relationships. If you don't have a boyfriend or husband, fill our your dreams in those slots. What do you want in a spouse?

Friends

Likes: ____

____

____

____

____

____

Dislikes:

____

____

____

____

____

Course of Action: ______________________________

____

____

____

____

____

Family

Likes:____

Dislikes:______________________________________

Course of Action: ______________________________

Co-Workers

Likes: _______________________________________

____

____

Dislikes: ____________________________________

____

____

____

____

Course of Action: ____________________________

____

____

____

____

____

You have the control inside you to change what you don’t like about your life, and although you can’t control others, there are changes you can make to each and every one of the above relationships to improve your satisfaction with them.

7 DEPRESSION

DEPRESSION HAS many levels, many contributing factors, and many symptoms. Everyone experiences depression at some point in his or her life. It happens. It's happened before, and it will probably happen again. That's just life. So, like anything else, we need to learn tactics to help cope with our depression. Though there are multitudes of reasons for depression, we will deal mostly with depression that began with relinquishment.

Relinquishment depression ranked alongside the death of a loved one as the worst depression I've ever had. I have never felt worse in my entire life. Truth be told, I probably needed medication during that time and I don't know why I never got any. Maybe it was because I had tried anti-depressants in the past and they made me feel like a zombie. I'm not sure, but maybe I should've given them another chance. Instead, I stayed depressed for nearly two years. It didn't help that seven months after my relinquishment my grandma died. She had always been my biggest support and lifeline here on earth. So believe me when I tell you – I *know* what it's like to be at the very bottom of the pit with junk piling in on top of you. I've hit rock bottom a few times in my life, and I'm the lucky one. Many other people struggle much more severely on a regular basis.

I've heard stories of people who live most of their lives in this type of deep, ongoing depression. It's very gripping, and as with any disease, they have had to learn to cope on a daily basis. Sometimes it is one day or one moment at a time. Once you are depressed, the steps are alike to try to beat it. If you feel medication will help your symptoms of depression, go to your doctor and get evaluated. Keep in mind, though, that for every pill we take, there are also side effects which also need to be taken into consideration.

The problems arise when we believe medications are the end-all-be-all for depression. I don't agree with this at all. I do not believe we should go get a prescription for things, hoping for it to alleviate us from having to help ourselves. Anti-depressants (or any pills) are only a portion of the answer.

I have a blood sugar issue and I know when I eat a lot of junk food or don't exercise, I feel *horrible* for days on end. Depression is the same way. There are habits that make it worse and there are habits that make it better. The more diligent we can be in our daily good habits, the more improvement or relief we will experience. Hopefully, you are already practicing a few good habits, including: daily prayer (meditation directed toward God), journaling, positive thinking, and daily fellowship with God.

These four habits, discussed in earlier chapters, will pay a return of peace, less anxiety (in my case), and better emotional and spiritual health. Much of the world recognizes the value of quiet meditation in emotional health. I have never understood meditation without God, though. Worldly meditation teaches us to focus on anything. I say, focus on God. He is the only One who can actually help, so why would you meditate on anything else?

Our physical health is obviously another important issue surrounding depression. It is a known fact that if we take care of ourselves emotionally, we feel better physically. Well, that also works in reverse. Physical activity stimulates various brain chemicals that may leave you feeling happier and more relaxed than you were before you worked out. You'll also look better and feel better when you exercise regularly, which can boost your confidence and improve your self-esteem. Regular physical activity can even help prevent depression.[7]

Our bodies were created to move. An anti depressant cannot fix that urge, that necessity. The only fix is to get up and move, whether we want to or not. I don't have a supermodel body, it's nothing special, but it does love exercise. Mind you, I don't particularly like doing it, but my body thanks me afterward. My mood, self-image, my confidence – they are all impacted by exercising. I can see a huge difference when I go a while without it. The truth is that our bodies ALWAYS crave movement, but after years of not moving, we just lose the ability to recognize the craving. When you first start out, it is hard. It is exhausting. It just plain stinks, but it pays off big time. If nothing else, it gets your mind off of your grief for a bit.

I'm sure you have heard of or maybe even known someone who had a problem with "cutting". People who do that say the reason is because the physical sensation of the cut takes their minds off of the emotional pain. Exercising, for me anyway, was an outlet much like cutting. When I am feeling stressed out, angry, aggressive, whatever the mood, I go take it out on my body with exercise. Those are some of my best workouts ever. While cutting is a very, very unhealthy way of releasing pain, I do get the idea behind it. It makes perfect sense! Take it to the treadmill instead, baby! Bring on those "feel good" hormones released during physical exertion.

My oldest son, Kasey, is allergic to many foods – especially fast food. If he would eat the wrong thing, it would cause him to have seizures. Now it triggers migraines. Well, before we figured this out, I was a junk food junkie. I wanted junk all the time. However, because of Kasey, we cut off all fast food. It was like a drug to me. Talk about having major withdrawals. I was miserable. What I noticed, after being off of it for a while, was that when I would eat it, it just didn't taste as good as I remembered and the day after eating it, I was an emotional train wreck.

When I was younger, my mom would always say, "You are grouchy! It's all that junk you ate yesterday!" I always thought she was just crazy. Until I totally cleaned my body out and began re-introducing it to healthy food, my husband avoided me like the plague and my kids peeked out from under the couch at me, teeth chattering and all! Now that's a bit of an exaggeration but you get my point. Who would think a simple cheeseburger, fries, and cola could instill deep fear inside my loved ones? That's when I realized that I really did have a problem. My point here is that we really are what we eat. It does make a difference.

1 Corinthians 3:16 ESV says: "Do you not know that you are God's temple and that God's Spirit dwells in you?"

God's Holy Spirit dwells within us. Our bodies are His temple! We need to take care of ourselves for Him, for ourselves, and for our loved ones. For many people, health is not very important until they no longer have it. Don't let this be the case for you. Healing involves a holistic approach. Holistic approaches require working on our mind, body, and soul. I studied nursing before I decided to enter ministry. What I learned from my years in that field is that it really is a miracle that we make it through each day physically. So many things have to happen inside our bodies each minute in order to keep us going. Even if one little thing is askew, it affects other parts of the body, other organs, hormones. It has a trickle-down effect. That is why it is so very critical to do what you can while you still have your health.

I used to work on a cancer unit and I saw first-hand the balance of soul, body, and mind required to conquer disease. Getting sick, even depression, is not for the faint of heart. It requires diligence and effort on our part. If you don't have your health, it is very critical to start utilizing whatever habits you can to improve what is left. I have heard of people completely turning around disease processes by changing their habits. It is worth it!

We need to choose *wisely* what we put into our bodies. As we make better choices, our spirits will lift. I have trouble with anxiety; I have most of my life. So, caffeine and sugar affect me in bad ways. I will consume caffeine once in a while, but I do it knowing that in a few hours I will feel like crawling out of my own skin. My anxiety levels rise and I get short of breath. Anxiety and depression are linked. It makes sense. I get tired of being anxious and it depresses me. Depression can also be a cause of anxiety. Some of you may be able to relate. Every decision, every day, *does* matter. Let's make our decisions matter for good.

Let me tell you two challenges I am running in to while writing this book: 1) actually conveying your *immense* worth, and 2) having you grab hold of that worth and accept it. I want you to overcome your depression, your past, your strongholds, and/or your relinquishment, but you have to be the one to work on accepting your worth and value as a child of God, a child with a purpose. *You* have to be the one to utilize all the tools in this book to feel better. I am happy to stock your tool shed, but unless you use the tools, nothing changes. As a whole, I hope that many women read this book. Individually, I hope each and every person reading this finishes with renewed value, restored hope for their future, and a peace and calm surpassing all understanding. I hope by the end of this book (or even sooner) that God has revived your lowly spirit. However, just like taking a pill can't fix every problem, neither can sitting back and expecting God to do all the work. You have to do the work *with* Him.

Another thing to consider for grief is counseling. Sometimes we need someone to help us sort our feelings and help clear the fog from our brains, someone who is a third party to the situation. This can be very cathartic. You need to do whatever it takes to get your feet on solid ground again. When looking for a therapist or counselor, one very important consideration is whether or not their counseling is biblically based. As I've stated before, God is ultimately the *only* way to complete any total healing, not to mention eternity. Stick with Him, honey. He is the Ultimate Counselor. He will never let you down.

Psalm 73:24 says, You guide me with Your counsel, and afterward You will take me into glory."

Write out the following verses about our Heavenly Counselor:

Isaiah 28:29: ______________________________

____

____

____

How much more could we ask for? A Wonderful Counselor, magnificent in wisdom.

Isaiah 9:6: __________________________________

____

____

____

____

Wonderful Counselor, Mighty God, Everlasting Father, Prince of Peace. Soak that in for a few minutes…Prince of Peace…you need peace, right? We all could use some!

John 14:26: __________________________________

____

____

The Counselor, the Holy Spirit, remember this from a few paragraphs ago? 1 Corinthians 3:16 ESV, "Do you not know that you are God's temple and that God's Spirit dwells within you?" His Spirit *is* within us when we believe in Him! The Holy Spirit is our built-in Counselor. The Holy Spirit teaches us all things and reminds us of everything spoken in the

Bible.

Psalm 16:7: ________________________________

____

____

____

Even in the darkness, He is there. Many times His instructions come in the form of a little thing called our "conscience." The more aware we are of what is on our consciences, the better. I know it doesn't feel great at the time, but listen anyway. Earlier I talked about how if you ignore your body's cravings for exercise enough, you will lose the ability to recognize the craving. So it is with our consciences. If we ignore it enough, we recognize it less. That is a big problem. I pray that God will ease your anguish and honor your perseverance and commitment to healing.

8 DISAPPOINTMENT

IT HAS not escaped me that this week as I sit down to write this chapter, I have been dealing with many *shoulda, coulda, woulda's*. Irony? I think not. God is funny like that. I wish I could tell you that dealing with disappointment is a one-time only deal. However, like so many things in life, it sneaks up on us every once in a while. We must have perseverance and be mentally equipped to conquer it. Satan likes to use this one on me.

Think about your past and present for a minute. Where does your disappointment lie? In what area(s) does it show up? What seems to trigger those disappointed feelings? Once you feel disappointed, how do you handle it? Does it crush you or does it make you push harder for success?

I generally feel pretty well about my past until I

mention it to someone and they get that look in their eyes or their demeanor changes. Sometimes, I even cause my own grief by pondering decisions made that can never be changed. By far, though, I experience the biggest disappointment relapses when I begin to measure my life using everyone else as the yardstick with which I measure. This is wrong on so many levels and I know that, yet, I find myself doing it still. I begin thinking, "Well, she did it this way," or, "she married *then* had kids," or, "She did everything right, she looks right, she acts right, she looks so put together, she is so well-spoken," and the list goes on and on. You know what I am talking about, right? The more inches I give everyone else, the shorter I get and the smaller I feel. This continues for me until I wonder why anyone would listen to what I have to say, want to be around me, respect me, be married to me, or anything else for that matter.

I worry how my kids will feel about me once they are at an age when they can fully grasp my past. That thought really gets me. I tell you, I *really* know how to beat myself up. What I have learned, though, is that I need to love myself and be okay with myself before anyone else will do the same. That's not a guarantee for good treatment, but it sure helps. Just yesterday, I was feeling down on myself. My husband and I were going somewhere and when he turned the car on, the radio was playing a song about Christ's love for us and immediately I felt calm and peaceful again. My identity is now rooted in Christ and I am enough to Him. I am loved. Am I like Do-it-all Doris? No. Am I like Hot Tamale Helen? Nope. Am I like Supermom Susan? Not really. We all know someone like these women, right? I am, however, becoming who God intended me to be and I have the gifts (ingrained in me and my personality) that God intended for me.

Oftentimes, we measure our disappointments up against invisible standards. The way society has said we *should* be, we *should* look, we *should* ___________ right? This is not healthy. The older I get, the more I realize that all the *shoulds* I have placed on myself are just plain stupid. When religion is stripped down to the very core, all that matters is who I am in Christ and what kind of relationship I have with Him. Let me tell you: He does not care how you dress, how much money you make, if you are tattooed or pierced, if you drink a glass of wine or if you wear a purple Mohawk! Societal norms don't matter to Him. He looks at your heart. He loves you right now, right where you are.

To feel disappointment is healthy to a degree, because it keeps us in line with our own consciences and it keeps us true to our bodies and souls, but constant and deep disappointment are not a fun way to live! God wants you to stand tall in front of everyone and not cower. When you accept Christ into your heart, you are the Daughter of a King, and you have a mighty power inside you called the Holy Spirit. We can only accomplish those things that God desires for us to do when we rely on that power of the Holy Spirit. It's a road we follow individually and we all reach our milestones at different times, just like infants learn to do things at different times.

When I was going through my adoption, I felt

used up and worthless. I felt like no one would ever want me and that my adoption would be a black mark on my life's record. Now that I have seen more of the picture, I realize my adoption has become a propellant for my life's purpose. Adoption gave me some knowledge to help me become what I was created to be. What I was created to be is a propellant for God's purpose. What I was created to be was someone who helps the hurting and cares about others. Not just the ones that look right or act right. God loves everyone and He has a plan for everyone. That plan already took into account our failures.

Although we don't think of this aspect often, even the quirks in our personalities that our parents tried to beat out of us can be used for God. I have a rebelliousness about me and when I was younger, all it took was someone telling me, "No," or, "You can't," to light a fire inside me to do just what I was told not to. That trait proved to be extremely self destructive when I was younger. My rebelliousness didn't just disappear when I accepted Jesus into my heart. No way, that would be too easy. Instead, it is being replaced with something I cherish and enjoy! It has manifested now as my "driving spirit". It drives me to become better. It drives me to prove to those who said, "No way Cynthia will ever amount to anything," that I can, I will, and I have, because of a God who is in the business of restoration. He is bigger than my past and He is raising me up to be bigger than my past. I haven't accomplished one thing without God, but I know He gave me certain traits that assist with accomplishing things. In the past, my rebellion caused me much disappointment.

Now that my "rebellion" is under God's authority, it manifests in a healthier, more playful way. I don't like fitting molds. It bores me. If someone expects me to do something one way, I will do it another just to keep things lively and fun, but in a loving way. My Christ-centered rebelliousness doesn't believe every word out of every teacher or preacher's mouth. I have to research it myself. My Christ-centered rebelliousness allows me to serve and worship with abandon, passion, and fire, even if it's not cool. My Christ-centered rebelliousness allows me opportunities to reach others that "religious" people would never say a warm hello to. That's only one personality flaw that God has turned around for me!

The world sees our flaws and judges us by them. God sees our flaws and waits patiently until we turn them over to Him for an adjustment. Every flaw we have becomes more and more reason for us to need Jesus. Every reason we have to need Jesus becomes a stair step to our success in life.

Success (and I don't mean the monetary kind) and blessings are never gained without disappointment along the way. Just last week, my good friend, Amanda, was sitting in a hospital room with her four year old son, waiting to see if it was his time to go home to Jesus or if she got to keep him for a while longer. For him to survive his ordeal, it would literally have to be a miracle. There was nothing more this world could do for him.

He went home from the hospital today, as if

nothing had ever happened to him. He should *not* be alive right now. When I talked to her, she said, "As upset as I've been through it all, it has been so amazing to witness such a miracle. I'm happy…"
This mommy got her miracle! Everyone wants miracles. The sheer fact that you are hoping and praying for a miracle means that something bad is going on in your life. The biggest blessings in life sometimes hurt a lot at first. Adoption hurts. Empty arms hurt. Separation from a child hurts. Let me assure you, though, a rainbow is on its way.

The ones who hold on to the *hope* of success even through the disappointments become the successful ones. Romans 5:5 tells us: "And hope does not disappoint us because God has poured out His love into our hearts by the Holy Spirit whom He has given us.

Remember the yardstick I measure myself with? In reality, my yardstick reaches to the heavens and into eternity. That's what matters. All along my life's path, I've encountered times where I've thought, "This is it, This is as good as it's going to get for me. This is where my yardstick ends and it's nowhere near the height of anyone else's." Yet, something inside me kept pushing me – as if saying, "Keep looking Honey, your yardstick really *is* bigger; you just can't see it because of the cloud in your way."

There were times I told myself, "You are crazy to believe better things are in store for you. You are nothing. And you never will be." Yet I kept hoping. Hope will pull you out of disappointment. Love yourself and don't let others pull you down. We are all individuals and God has different plans for each individual soul. Don't measure yourself based on others! It's not a fair comparison.

I had a family member once tell me that no one would ever want to take on my "baggage". To him it just wasn't going to happen. A quick explanation: "baggage" was another word for a single mother with a special needs son and his little brother, both with different fathers. No, neither had the same father as Joshua, the son I relinquished. However, one of the two babies I aborted shared the same father as Joshua. Yep, I'd say that is some serious baggage. More importantly, none of it was matching. Every woman inherently knows that matching baggage is a much better way to go, right? Humor is another essential to getting through life's tough seasons. Ok, let's be serious!

Can you see how I could be just a little disappointed in myself? Anyway, when I was dating my future husband, Eric, I told him all about my baggage right away because I didn't want to waste my time with someone who couldn't deal with it. I took him to meet this family member who had said these things and, of course, the family member said the same thing to Eric. Talk about a stab in the gut. That hurt!

Without flinching, Eric told him (in my words), "I've got lots of baggage, too, and mine doesn't match either!" Let me tell you, ladies, I *never* expected my knight in shining armor to be as good as Eric is! If

I could have sat down and made up a list of characteristics the perfect man would have, I still wouldn't have gotten him as close to perfect as God did. The real shocker is this – He did it all without my help! That's only one area in my life I assumed my failures had ruined.

Sometimes I will remember something from my past that I had forgotten and will instantly feel shame over it. I've done some incredibly stupid things and made some incredibly bad decisions. What's key for me is to immediately turn it over to God and ask His forgiveness (don't forget to forgive yourself also!) and thank Him for His saving grace. As I like to put it, "The world can be pretty unforgiving, but God isn't, so live on, Baby!" Our disappointments can hold us down like a bug under a shoe or they can propel us to a great, passion-filled life. Just as you chose adoption for your precious little one you can choose hope for yourself. Hope does not disappoint.

As I stated back in the first chapter, there was one person I was afraid to let down. I let that man down so many times it isn't even funny, and I would've rather eaten worms than let him know I had done it again. That man is my step-dad. I experienced great disappointment just at the thought of telling him about my adoption. He came into my life when I was twelve and, of course, I thought he was the devil. How dare he come into my cozy little life! Yet, over the years and years of my nastiness toward him, he stayed constant. He still seemed to love me and care about me.

Now that I am an adult, I value him and his opinion very much. He stayed by me (and I'm sure there were many times he did not want to in the least) and seemed to love me in spite of myself.

We all have people we feel responsible to, and when we miss the mark, we feel it in our hearts. Don't beat yourself up. Be kind to yourself. Do what you need to try to rebuild any relationship that is meaningful to you. All you can do is your part and if there is no response from the other party, pray. Pray that God would soften their heart to you. Pray without ceasing!

I have some serious stuff to relay in this book and I do hope I am getting it across, but at the same time, I'm just me and I have a tendency to be silly. I don't know how to be anyone else. I still look in the mirror some days and wonder if I am ever going to feel like a grown up. I would say that, a good 95 percent of the time, people don't take me seriously and I'm okay with that. However, tell someone about your past, and they take you even less seriously.

Another "scar" I have is tattoos, and, outwardly, I don't look like much. If you judge me based on my appearance, you wouldn't guess me as the typical follower of Jesus. Most people, however, will immediately write me off with their eyes. Eyes truly are a window to the soul and, many times, they tell the truth more than our mouth does. I watch it happen. The funny thing is that people judge immediately, it's that first impression thing that I'm not very good at. Their first glance says it all – Boom:

you've been judged. For me it's, "She has a tattoo! Oh my Lord, please save her poor soul!" If any of you reading this have one, you get me! The second glance says: "Oh, wait a minute, Lord, please forgive me…her tattoo says, 'Daughter of A King, Isaiah 61'"…A few seconds of remorse and then…"Wait a second, in the Bible it says no tattoos." Voila, back into judgment mode. This is funny stuff, but I'm serious as a heart attack!

People will judge you. Even church people will do it, and they may do it worse. For the record, Jesus was not like that when He was on Earth. He was the same to everyone no matter who they were, whom they were associated with, or how they looked. He hung out with commoners and people "religious" folks labeled as outcasts and nobodies. I've seen many people leave churches with their heads rolling because they were unfairly judged. I am telling you this because I want you to realize that church people are human, too, and are not always good people.

Go to God. Ask Him to show you how He sees you. If you don't look weird, someone will find another reason somewhere down the line, and when it happens, you are going to need to know who you are and where your identity comes from or it will send you straight back to the land of disappointment and your yardstick will once again be shorter than everyone else's. If your identity is rooted in Christ, *no one* can steal you away from your King. No one can tell you that you are a disappointment or worthless or anything else. God would *never* tell you that. Don't believe *anyone* (whether they say they represent Christ or not) who tells you that you are not worth anything because of ________________ (fill in the blank). With Jesus, there is no, "I love you, but…". Only an, "I love you. Period. Just as you are."

I apologize if I offend you by calling out "religious" people, but what we don't always realize as followers of Christ is that we have an increased risk of doing more damage to people because others are looking to see Jesus in us. Even when we fall short (which we will), people are still looking for Jesus. That can cause major stumbling for people. Please remember that God's followers are still human and we make mistakes and when we do, don't take it to heart, take it to God. Allow Him to be the Hope that lifts your disappointment and turns it into your success.

Do you have anyone in your life that you hate letting down? ____

Does a fair amount of your disappointment ride on their opinion? ________________________________

Is there peace in this relationship(s) right now, and if not, what can you do to make peace on your end?

____

____

____

____

____

____

9 SEPARATION

HOW ARE you doing with feelings of separation from your baby? At what times does your decision cause you the most separation issues? This separation thing just doesn't seem natural, right? Not being able to look into your baby's eyes or stroke his/her tiny little cheeks or kiss them…I know.

Have you ever ended a relationship because it wasn't healthy? Remember the relief that came immediately? Then, if you are anything like me, a few months later you were sitting around actually having warm fuzzies about the whole thing? We tend to romanticize our lives when reflecting. Adoptions are the same way. They are hard. They rock you, even if you have strong resolve to stick with your decision. I had seriously strong resolve even in the midst of my heart breaking. I actually shocked myself at my strength. However, the more time that passed, the more I tended to look back on it and think, "I could have done it, I could have kept my son," I've had a few of those moments since my relinquishment.

My regrets snuck up on me quickly. I felt no doubt in my mind that adoption was right for my baby. Yet, give it a little time and even the strongest person will be tested. My doubts came in after I met my husband. He would have accepted my son Joshua. He is an awesome man of God. I met him one month after Joshua was born, and we were married a year and three months later. Because of glitches in the court system, Joshua's adoption was barely finalized by the time I was married.

Besides my gut feeling that adoption was right, the biggest personal reason I chose adoption was because his birthfather led a very questionable, wild lifestyle. My son would have been exposed to many things that even adults shouldn't be exposed to. I literally feared for Joshua's safety should I decide to keep him.

Joshua's birthfather died three years after I gave birth. More specifically, while I was in the middle of writing this book. So I was not only reliving Joshua's adoption in my writing, but grieving for my first love. Four months after his death, one of my oldest and closest friends died of cancer. Believe me, there were many times throughout this book that I wanted to quit writing. The thought of you and the pain of your bondage is what kept me pressing on. I hope that gives you a glimpse of my love and desire for you to become complete. Anyway, a family member asked me if the reason I was grieving his death so deeply was because I didn't have to give my son up. Well, that idea had not crossed my mind up to that point, but afterward, it crossed more than a few times. No one made me. I *chose* it based on knowledge and information I had at the time. Who knows what the future holds, right? Yet, I entertained the "what-ifs." You know the answer I got? God's plan is divine and He will take care of everyone involved.

I could have kept Joshua, but, had I chosen to, that one decision would have changed the whole course of events. I wouldn't be writing this book and I would either be in a toxic, abusive marriage or I would be a widow. Either way I look at it, it's grim. I'm happy to report that because I took this path, I am married to a Godly man and my soul flourishes now where it once was dead and barren. Because I am not busy patching and re-patching a toxic relationship, I can focus on my Father, my Savior, my Comforter. Because He and He alone causes my soul to leap for joy, I can pass that on to my children. All because of that one decision.

I still look in Joshua's eyes sometimes and it hurts me that he has no idea of the depth of the connection between us. I just think about the future he has. He has a mother *and* a father. I trust that they are both leading him in God's direction. Ultimately, my main desire is that we will see one another in heaven…and I will be reconciled to the child of my womb for eternity. Then, although there is so much I want to tell him, one thing I will never tell him again is goodbye.

Your life will continue on without your baby, and

at some point you *are* going to look back and realize that you could have raised a baby, that your situation is so much different and your relinquished child would fit perfectly into your new life. Just remember, if one decision in your past had changed, things would not be exactly the same. A good motto to live by is this: Make the best decisions you can given the knowledge and information you have available to you at the time and leave the rest up to God. He does not disappoint.

Separation is hard. It truly is taking a complete unit and dividing it. From what I can tell, women know in their hearts early on what is best for their situation; it's just whether or not they listen. Even if the decision is to parent, it takes will-power and resolve.

Fellowship with God is similar. He is (or wants to be) our Father. He wants our "separation" from Him to end and for us to be restored to Him. He wants to hold us in His arms and comfort us just like a father. His heart aches for us when we are away from Him. He longs for us and thinks about us constantly, just as we do for our children. We wonder about our children returning to us. Will they want anything to do with us when they become adults? We wait patiently for that glimmer of hope just as our Father in Heaven also waits…for us.

Revelation 3:20 ESV says, "Behold, I stand at the door and knock. If anyone hears My voice and opens the door, I will come in to him and eat with him, and he with Me."

Our Father longs for us to recognize Him the way we long for our babies to recognize us. He's standing at your door, longing for you to let Him in so He can fill your empty arms, mend your broken heart, dry your tears, and fulfill great things in your life. Dare to do for Him now what you want *your* child to do for you one day. He *will* put the smile back on your beautiful face!

10 ANXIETY/FEAR

ISAIAH 41:10 says, "So do not fear, for I am with you; do not be dismayed, for I am your God. I will strengthen you and help you; I will uphold you with my righteous right hand."

Anxiety is defined as a painful or apprehensive uneasiness of mind usually over an impending or anticipated ill."[8] Fears are essentially the same things. This chapter is a little more challenging for me because every woman's fears will be slightly different, but I will try to address the subject in general and how it pertained to my adoption.

Anxiety and fear are two emotions I've struggled with most of my life. When I am under stress, the symptoms of my anxiety get worse. After I came home from delivering Joshua, I was an anxious mess. I thought I was going to die from anxiety alone. I was anxious over where Joshua was and what he was doing. I was anxious over seeing loved ones for the first time since delivery, how they would react to me, and what they would say. I was anxious about keeping my emotions in check in front of people. I was anxious over all the physical and emotional pain I was experiencing. The weird thing was that on the outside you wouldn't have known it. It was all anxiety rooted deep inside my soul. One of my biggest fears was of losing control or going crazy, so I was not going to let anyone "see" my anxieties. I became very reclusive, staying at home a lot because my fears became gripping, always wondering if, when, where, how…I was fearful to live at that point.

I have a journal entry that says, "I don't want to die but I don't know how to live either," I was paralyzed with fear just at the thought of leaving my house.

Nowadays, I still have the tendency to be fearful, so every single day I have to give it over to God, take many deep breaths, and remember to enjoy every moment. God never intended for us to live in fear. If we are living in fear, we aren't really living.

As I addressed in an earlier chapter, we need to rest in the confidence of our God. We absolutely need to have faith in our God who is bigger than *any* problem or circumstance we face here on earth. If you are not at a point where you have faith in God, then at the very least you need to decide to have some faith in yourself. Have faith to reach for your dreams, have faith to stand tall amidst your brokenness, and have faith to rise above your past and your decisions so that you can become the best you possible.

Philippians 4:6-7 says, "Do not be anxious about anything, but in everything, by prayer and petition, with thanksgiving, present your requests to God. And the peace of God, which transcends all understanding, will guard your hearts and your minds in Christ Jesus."

I have a horrible memory, so Scripture memorization is not my specialty, but the essence of this verse is with me always. I still sometimes have panic attacks, and what pulls me out of them is to immediately stop the negative self-talk that is *always* going on in my mind right before the anxiety sets in. I call out to Jesus for help (not audibly, usually, but in silent prayer) and I remind myself to breathe deeply. That is my recipe for peace. Jesus is the essential ingredient for peace; the others are just the "spices".

Are you worried about where you go from here? What your future holds? I was too. The key is going to be in working through each of your fears individually, dissecting them to see if they are even valid fears or just imagined, made worse in your mind than they actually are or will be. All of life is about coping.

So is anxiety. Healthy coping mechanisms bring about relief and, as I've stated various other times throughout this book, journaling will help you deal with all emotions – anxiety included. Getting adequate "quiet time" every day will help. You already have the suggestion to get into God and your Bible daily. That's some excellent quiet time there. Meditate on God. I try to get up early for quiet time with my

Father God, and I can always tell the difference when I get it and when I don't.

Getting regular exercise, even just a short walk, will help you clear your head and calm down. Put your grief into exercise and watch for healthy results. You can almost literally feel your heart grow stronger, both physically and emotionally. It's as if your emotional baggage just begins dropping off with each step. I highly recommend exercise. You probably feel so heavily laden with grief that you don't want to move, but trust me, as you move and meditate on Jesus, you will feel lighter. We can't lie around hoping our problems dissipate. We *have* to be proactive in our own lives Because if we won't, who will?

I've heard it said that F.E.A.R. is nothing more than False Evidence Appearing Real. Think about that for a moment. It's true, isn't it? Almost every time I am fearful, it is an unreasonable fear that is more of a threat in my imagination than in reality. From as far back as I can remember I have always been a negative thinker – Catastrophizer, actually. What I have since learned is that negative thinking is nothing more than a bad habit that needs to be broken. The more we do it, the more we do it. Positive thinking, then, is exactly the same. So replace negative thoughts with a believable positive thought instead, then breathe deep and pray until the anxiety passes.

I win my anxiety battle daily and know that each day I win is one day closer to not having it at all. However, every single day my anxiety brings me closer to my God, the Controller and Creator of my life. He is the only way I make it through life. If I didn't need Him, would I seek Him? If I believed I had all the answers I need, would I draw close to Him? Every flaw is one more reason to show me my need for a savior.

1Peter 5:7 says, "Cast all your anxiety on Him because He cares for you."

Proverbs 12:25 says, "An anxious heart weighs a man down, but a kind word cheers him up."

Be kind to yourself. Allow God to show you His kindness and work on *truly* accepting it. Be anxious for nothing.

Read Matthew 6:25-34. How do these verses speak to you personally?

____

____

____

____

____

____

____

____

____

____

What can you do for yourself to help relieve any fears/anxieties you are having?

____

____

____

____

____

____

____

____

One thing I do know is that someday I will get my deliverance from fear and anxiety, and that is exciting to me! Especially since God reigns on high and I am seriously afraid of heights. Stick with your healing, you owe it to yourself. With each chapter you finish, more beauty will come from the ashes of your life. I'm right beside you through this and much more importantly, so is Jesus.

Let's pick through your fears a bit here.

What are you fearful or anxious about right now?

____

____

____

____

____

Are those fears reasonable? Why or why not?

What positive, believable thoughts can you meditate on to replace the negative, scary, and unreasonable thoughts? (Remember, they must be believable and not just happy.)

11 ANGER

EVEN BEFORE my adoption, I was angry. I was already in a situation that I was not happy with, yet I couldn't bring myself to change it. When I had a positive pregnancy test, it put me over the edge. At the time, I had an early morning class at the college and my teacher was, to say the least, a bubbly, perpetually happy human being. Not the sort a stale, perpetually unhappy person wants to be around, let alone converse with in the early morning hours. I dreaded those class days because her happiness could invoke such anger in me. There I sat week after week during my pregnancy. Unhappy people do not enjoy watching others enjoy life. I was angry at this teacher simply for being chipper and upbeat. How dare she enjoy living!! Irrational? Absolutely. However, angry people are often not very rational. For the record, this teacher is now my friend and I love her dearly. Back then, I just couldn't see past my own misery and I wanted everyone else to feel miserable too.

I was also angry at God. One journal excerpt I wrote said, "I am angry that you would ask me to do this! I feel like giving up and walking away from everything. Every time I manage to get up you crush me back down again…Help me…the anger and rage inside me burn deeply…Why don't you take me out of this fire? Replace my rage with love. Please do. I am begging you."

My anger was a hateful kind of anger. As I reflect back on that journal entry to God, I realize just how irrational it is. God wasn't making me do anything. I had a choice as to whether or not my son was adopted. God wasn't the one that crushed me down. I managed to do that all on my own. God wasn't the one that put me in the fire. Yet I blamed Him anyway. How could I really believe in my heart that God had done this to me? I made the choices for my own life. I put myself in a bad situation that resulted in my pain and grief. None of my thoughts on God's role in all of it were rational. I had single-handedly managed to cause my grief all on my own.

The rage inside my heart didn't exclude me, either. I hated everything about myself. Looking into the mirror disgusted me and looking into my own soul disgusted me even more. I hated the weak, pathetic girl that had gotten me into this situation. I hated my situation, but I also hated the change that would be needed to create a new one. I was not only mean and cruel in my actions, but I was also cruel to the very spirit inside of me.

Ephesians 4:26-27 says, "Be angry and do not

sin; do not let the sun go down on your anger, and give no opportunity to the devil."
Read those verses very carefully and then write what it means to you in your own words.

____

____

____

____

____

____

____

____

Notice the first two words: "Be angry." Anger is not the problem. Anger is an everyday emotion. The things that our anger causes us to do are the real problems. I know that almost every time I get angry, I want to do something destructive, I have to stop myself dead in my tracks to stay in line with my conscience and my character. We need to be real with ourselves regarding this emotion and really grasp on to it. We may be angry but we must not let the anger control our actions. It is also okay to get real with God regarding your anger. He is a kind and compassionate God. He is willing to experience any and every bit of emotion life has to offer with us. All we have to do is communicate with Him and listen for a response. You are not going to push Him away with your feelings, nor will you anger Him by being open and transparent with Him. He will never give up on you so get real with Him. He prefers us to be open and transparent.

Now look at the last part of those verses: "do not let the sun go down on your anger, and give no opportunity to the devil." You've probably heard that one said before. Don't let the sun go down on your anger. So many people quote it, so few do it. Stamp this on your heart, for not only is it good in general, it is also good for your health (both physical and emotional). Don't be afraid to say you're sorry. Don't sit around waiting for someone else to say it first. Lead by example. Isn't it always that after a huge storm blows through there is some cleaning up to do? It is the same with the storms of our hearts. I know that every time I have lost my cool, I have to go back and do damage control; trying to clean up all the debris (whether words or actions) of my outburst. Unfortunately, much of the damage is permanent. Whether it was intended or accidental, one thing is for sure: words and actions cannot be taken back.

James 1:19-20 says; "Everyone should be quick to listen, slow to speak and slow to become angry, for man's anger does not bring about the righteous life that God desires."

When dealing with extreme emotions like anger in grief, it is important to try to redirect that anger in constructive ways. Anger is a normal aspect of life, but this is especially true during times of grief. We want to blame someone else or ourselves, or maybe even God. For our own sake, forgiveness will be key to our peace and calm. We need to evaluate our anger.

Keep in mind, we don't offer forgiveness to others to let them off the hook. Instead, we offer it to lighten our hearts and minds. We offer forgiveness to others for our own sake. We've been taught that milk is what does a body good, but actually, forgiveness does too.

I wish I could tell you the exact moment I became a happy-happy, joy-joy kind of person, but I can't.

My journey down anger ally changed slowly as I began making better choices, thinking more positively, changing circumstances, changing the things I did not like about my life, forgiving myself and others, and dealing with my anger towards God. Let's also not get lazy about our crowd -- we should seek out wise and joyful people to do life with. You will never believe it until you try it, but sometimes a crowd change is just what is needed for a positive and calm outlook on life. Ask God to help you replace your rage with love. I didn't realize how profound that was at the time I wrote it. The connection between love and anger is monumental.

My anger dissipated each day that I looked in the mirror and decided to truly love the woman staring back at me unconditionally. Ironically, it was the very same unconditional love I had been expecting someone else to give me all these years. The same love our Heavenly Father has for us. It is amazing how something as simple as love can take away fear, calm anxieties, soothe anger, and lighten the load on our hearts. Yet, it truly does!

We have to start somewhere on our journey to recovery and I hope that love permeates your whole journey. Love yourself, every day. In those moments when you don't like what you see, change it, so that you can love that part too.

I truly love you and care about your recovery, and I don't even know you. How much more does your Father in Heaven, who sees you in your entirety. Stick it out with Him!

Have you experienced anger since your adoption?

____

____

____

What are the things that trigger your anger?

____

____

____

____

____

____

____

____

Is there someone you need to forgive in your adoption situation? Is it yourself?

____

____

____

____

____

____

____

____

12 HELPLESSNESS

ALL OF the previous chapters are about teaching you to believe in yourself, trusting God, and empowering you to make better choices in the future. The theme and message delivered in this chapter may seem a bit like an oxymoron but stay with me here.

When I feel helpless, I get fearful. During my adoption, I was more helpless than I thought I had ever been. I felt helpless on every level. I couldn't fix my grief, I couldn't take my own pain away. I was helpless to hold my baby or trace his lips with my fingers, or hold his tiny, little hand until his fingers curled around mine. Still yet, on a more immediate level, I was helpless to care for the children I already had. I was helpless to provide basic care for myself. I knew that, alone, I was never going to come out of this trial alive. My spirit was weak and broken.

I was raised around church, not really in one exactly, but my grandmothers loved God with all their hearts. One thing they relayed to me was that nothing we do is a complete success unless God is involved. I knew about God for much of my life, but wasn't really interested in following all the rules He seemed to have, and being "boring". For most of my young life, I believed that I could have fun and then find God again later. What happened is that I did have my fun, but it wasn't really as fun as I thought it would be.

Actually, it was not fun at all. It only brought pain and heartache. By not following the rules, and instead doing things my way, I felt powerful. What happened was that the more I relied only on myself, the more dependent and helpless I became. With each rebellious decision I made, I actually gave up more freedom in my life. Pretty soon, my rebellious decisions had me locked into parenting, being responsible for someone else's life, and not just anyone's life, a helpless, dependent child's life.

Their lives depended on my success or failure. At an early age, my life became hard, as I was sexually abused around the age of four. Everything from there on became my (a helpless, dependent child) trying to survive in a grown-up world. I was surrounded by adult content a good majority of the time. As a result, I have always felt a strong conviction that when I did have children, they were going to be loved and protected fiercely.

I have three children now: my two sons that I chose to parent, and Joshua, my birth child. I can honestly say, without a shadow of a doubt, that I have loved and protected each of them just as fiercely. I just chose different methods. By placing Joshua with his adoptive parents, I loved him enough to want a healthy environment for him to be nurtured in.

All three of my children were helpless and relied solely on me. So who do we, as adults, rely on when we are helpless? Does it depend on the situation? Is it family or friends? Is it even someone reliable? I have been reduced to helplessness and tears many times in my life and there is only One that has consistently helped with each and every situation. Friends and family are wonderful, don't get me wrong. However, it isn't either of those. There is only One God, One Creator of the universe, and He is truly the only One that can be of eternal, everlasting help. My friends and family helped me get through the tough times of adoption, but nothing brought more peace to my situation than God. He's the only One that has the power to change things.

Psalm 10:14 says, "But you, oh God, do see trouble and grief; you consider it to take it in hand. The victim commits himself to you; you are the helper of the fatherless."

"Fatherless" doesn't just mean our earthly fathers, our step-fathers, our adoptive fathers. If we are void of our Spiritual Father, we are alone, no matter how many people surround us. This passage isn't just saying He is a helper once in a while. He is a helper every day, all day. When we really get down to the basics of life, the essentials, we are completely helpless. We can't control when we die, we can't control if, when, and how illness is going to affect us. We can't really control anything to a very large degree. We can help on a minute, small scale. We need to face it, we are powerless. We are helpless here on earth – from infancy to old age. Who then do we turn to? How do we find peace in the midst of this helplessness?

It is an everyday surrender. We have to learn to relinquish power to God. Now, with that, please don't misunderstand that we have power until we give it up to God. We don't ever truly have the power, we just think we do. Part of having a surrendered heart to Jesus is giving Him everything. Our fears, our hopes, our helpless situations – total control over our lives. He's already got the control; show Him you are ready to rest in it. Give your helplessness wings, let it flutter from your heart to lift the burden and become the most healthy dependency in the history of man; the dependency on a God who will carry you daily through the rest of your life. He is a God of hope that will never leave you or forsake you.

Look at Hebrews 13:5-6: "…Never will I leave you; never will I forsake you. So we say with confidence, 'The Lord is my helper; I will not be afraid…'"

Do not fear; you are in good hands. Rest. Rest in your Father's arms. There is no better place to be.

Are you feeling helpless in any way right now?

____

____

____

____

____

____

____

Does feeling helpless invoke any other feelings inside you?

____

____

____

____

____

____

____

____

13 JEALOUSY

GALATIANS 5:19-26 says, 'The acts of the sinful nature are obvious: sexual immorality, impurity and debauchery, idolatry and witchcraft; hatred, discord, jealousy, fits of rage, selfish ambition, dissensions, factions and envy; drunkenness, orgies, and the like. I warn you, as I did before, that those who live like this will not inherit the kingdom of God. But the fruit of the Spirit is love, joy, peace, patience, kindness, goodness, faithfulness, gentleness and self-control. Against such things there is no law. Those who belong to Christ Jesus have crucified the sinful nature with its passions and desires. Since we live by the (Holy) Spirit, let us keep in step with the Spirit. Let us not become conceited, provoking and envying each other.'

As I was typing these Scriptures, I realize just how many of those sinful acts applied to my adoption, not to mention the many that have woven their way through the fabric of the rest of my life. The reality of it stings a bit. As you read over this passage, did you feel a bit convicted like I did? I am only focusing on jealousy here, though.

As I stated previously, I was intensely jealous of Joshua's adoptive parents. I hated the fact that they would hit all the milestones with him, wake up to his smiling face, see him take his first steps, be on the receiving end of his "mommies," and comfort him when he hurts. My heart told me those were my privileges. My mind reminded me that they were not. My heart would melt at the thought of those milestones, and my mind would ice it over again.

I had prayed for wisdom choosing the best parents for Joshua. I had diligently done my homework and made sure I was 100 percent positive that this couple was the couple. I had chosen them because I liked them, yet, when the rubber met the road, I was envious of them. Truth be told, sometimes I felt hatred for them. While grieving my loss, I was trying to pull back the curtains of my heart to let light in, but when I would start thinking on these things, darkness would settle in again. It was almost as if I could watch it happen. I could feel it happen. It was not pretty.

To overcome this jealousy, we need a thankful heart. We need to be reminded of what God has chosen for us. We need to journal. We need physical reminders of what we do have. We need those reminders daily, sometimes hourly. Find yourself some quiet time soon, and begin writing what you are thankful for. I didn't actually write mine out when I was going through it, but I started with the basics. "Okay Jesus…thank you that I woke up breathing today?...Thank you for sunshine?...Thank you that I actually have air to breath, food to eat, a roof over my head, a car that gets me places?..." You get the picture.

I used question marks for those examples because, even as I was speaking them, I was still trying to convince myself to be thankful. We have to find the good in everything. That is my challenge to you this week. Don't be a pessimist, but instead be thankful. The more thankful you are, the less jealous you will become. These are two emotions that don't play well together.

In regards to your adoption, focus on what you do have. What do you have with your child? Maybe it is an open adoption, so there is plenty of hope for future relations. Maybe it is a closed adoption and there is hope for contact when your child is older. No matter the situation, there is some reason for hope. Find it. The good thing is that in today's society, adoptions are not as "sealed off" as they used to be. There is more hope these days for contact and more ways to get into contact. You may very well not be the only jealous one in this adoption circle.

Please be sensitive to that, also. I don't know this to be fact. I am simply stating how I think I would feel as an adoptive parent. I would be jealous that another woman created my child, carried it in her womb, nurtured it for months on end, and was caring enough to give it to another person out of love.

Adoptive parents are the ones who jump through hoops just to be able to be considered for a baby. There is not one that wants to give a child to someone else. They fully understand the sacrifice made for them whether they acknowledge it or not. However, jealousy on either end is not healthy. I wanted to bring that to light just so you remember that the special bond you have to your child is one that you share with no one. Be thankful for that. It is precious. The umbilical cord is the eternal tie.

When I was in nursing school, I went to a cadaver lab once. This is where you go down to the "dungeon" to look at all aspects of a dead body. I learned so many fascinating things at that lab, but the one thing I remember the most is that the eighty-year-old female cadaver still had her umbilical cord attached to the underside of her belly button! I was so impressed that, eighty years later, she still had the cord that linked her to her mother in utero. That cord had once nourished her, helped her develop, helped give her life. It was integral to her becoming who she was created to be. The life on the other end of that cord was her birthmother…

Isn't that just what God wants to be to us? He wants to be our umbilical cord! He wants to nourish us, help us develop, and give us life in its most pure and truest form! Once we are born in Him, no matter where life takes us, we still show evidence of His presence in our lives. Be thankful, dear birthmother. Your award is prestigious, for no matter where life takes you, no matter how far it may take you from the child of your womb, the evidence of your presence in his/her life is still woven inside their very being. God has been watching your heartache and grieving with you. He will bring it full circle. Not only do I believe He will bring you full circle, I also believe He will honor your decision and bring forth blessings abundant for both you and your child. Wait upon the Lord.

Have you felt jealousy over your adoption?

____

What/Who have you felt it toward?

____

____

____

____

____

____

____

____

What are you going to do with that jealousy now?

____

____

____

____

Romans 15:13 says, "I pray that the God who gives hope will fill you with much joy and peace while you trust in Him."

14 STEPPING OUT

HERE WE are. We have hit the final chapter of our journey together. How are you feeling?

____

____

____

____

____

____

Are you beginning to stand taller and look the world in the eyes? Is your burden beginning to lift? And are you feeling lighter. Explain.

____

____

____

____

____

____

Matthew 11:28-30 says: "Come to me, all you who are weary and burdened, and I will give you rest. Take my yoke upon you and learn from me, for I am gentle and humble in heart, and you will find rest for your souls. For my yoke is easy and my burden is light." These are Jesus' words. He is talking to you.

Sit for a few moments to soak that in and then write down how that makes you feel.

____

____

____

____

____

____

____

____

Ephesians 1:7 says: "In Him we have redemption through His blood, the forgiveness of sins, in accordance with riches of God's grace…"

I thank God for the forgiveness of my sins. Don't you? I would be floundering around right now if it weren't for His mercy and forgiveness.

Look up Ephesians 1:18-19 and write it here:

____

____

____

____

____

____

____

How do you feel about this verse?

____

____

____

____

____

____

____

Revelation 21:7 tells us: "He who overcomes will inherit all this, and I will be his God and He will be my son."

With Christ, you have the power to overcome your adoption. Your inheritance awaits you in heaven. God's child, how sweet the sound.

Now look up Ephesians 2:10 and write it here.

____

____

____

____

____

____

____

Does your mind believe this verse? How about your heart? Many times in life, my mind and heart are divided. Getting them on the same page requires diligence. Own these verses as your own. Even if it's only in your mind at first, it will eventually make its way to your heart. This is your Heavenly Father speaking directly to you in all of these!

Philippians 1:6 tells us to be confident of this: "…that He who began a good work in you will carry it on to completion until the day of Christ Jesus."

What does this mean in your situation?

____

____

____

____

____

Philippians 4:19 says, "And my God will meet all your needs according to His glorious riches in Christ Jesus."

Write out John 10:10:

____

____

____

____

____

Jesus gave His life so you could have life – and not just any life but a full life. He doesn't want you to constantly grieve and/or simply exist, He wants you to thrive.

John 6:47 explains how we gain eternal life in Jesus: "I tell you the truth, he who believes has everlasting life."

Do you believe in God? Do you believe in Jesus? Do you believe in the Holy Spirit?

____

____

Are you ready to surrender your life to Him (if you haven't already)?

____

Surrender is of key importance to your

relationship with God. Furthermore, your relationship with God is of key importance to surviving and thriving in the midst of your adoption.

I once wrote a list of what birthmothers are and what they are not. Own what you truly are, burying it deep inside you as fertilizer for your soul. Cast off what you are not and let no one tell you different.

What a birthmother is not:
She is not a piece of trash.
She is not a failure.
She is not a lost cause.
She is not a bad or unfit mother.
She is not all used up.

What a birthmother is:
She is human.
She is a sinner (like everyone else).
She is forgiven.
She is a vessel Jesus has and can use again.
She is blessed.
Most importantly…she is the daughter of the King.

Hold unswervingly to hope because He who has promised is faithful!

There will be days, especially in the first year, that you grieve. Anniversary reactions are very common. It's okay to grieve. Yet, for yourself, keep moving forward. Keep working towards restoration. I had a day not long ago that I just cried and cried for the losses I've experienced in the last four years. I was apologizing profusely to Christ for still grieving these losses. I had powerful sobs coming from deep inside my soul. The answer He gave me was that it was okay. I had experienced great loss in four years time and if I had a day I just wanted to fall apart, it was okay . As long as I allowed joy in the morning…and it came. Morning brought with it the sweet fragrance of life that Jesus had planted in my heart during the night.

Whenever I see a vase, I think of all the things it represents to me: beauty, a creator's love, passion, and purity. Vases are a very simple idea, yet contain so much diversity. I imagine the hours and love put into each one to make it exactly what it is supposed to be. Yet, as I said before, with cracks it cannot fulfill its purpose. It cannot contain the exact things it was created to hold – beautiful, fragrant flowers. Vases were created to hold life…how is your vase looking? My wish for you is that your vase is now home to life. May it resemble beauty, a Creator's love, passion, and purity. May His Spirit in your vase emit an aroma more magnificent and splendid than any flower could ever produce. Father, let it be an aroma so sweet that everyone around wants it too. Live on, sweet girl. Your life is just beginning…

Prayer of Salvation

Father, I ask you to come in to my heart.
I believe in you and I love you!
Please forgive me of all my sins.
I know that I am not worthy but I
Thank you for loving me in spite of myself.
I confess you as Lord of my life and I thank you for the redemption I have in you! Amen.

Now that you have prayed this prayer, continue on in your search for Christ including getting plugged in to a church that suits you and getting baptized. Baptism is an outward sign of your commitment to Christ. Jesus loves you, sweet girl, so continue pressing on!

ABOUT THE AUTHOR

Cynthia and her husband Eric reside in the Longmont, CO area with their two boys. She is not only a birthmother herself, but she has also counseled women through adoptions and crisis pregnancies. She holds a Bachelor's degree in Ministry. Her inspiration came when God revealed to her how many broken, hurting women never come full circle in their adoptions. Her hope is that this book will be a resource for birthmothers to use in healing relinquishment grief and finding happiness and wholeness in Christ Jesus.

Contact information is:
cynthia@cynthiachristensen.com

REFERENCES

1. www.merriam-webstercollegiate.com
2. www.merriam-webstercollegiate.com
3. www.merriam-webstercollegiate.com
4. www.merriam-webstercollegiate.com
5. www.grantsgraceland.org. Tim Storey, September 26th quote
6. www.merriam-webstercollegiate.com
7. www.mayoclinic.com/health/exercise/HQ01676
8. www.merriam-webstercollegiate.com

www.ingramcontent.com/pod-product-compliance
Lightning Source LLC
Chambersburg PA
CBHW022113280326
41933CB00007B/363

9780692453162